W9-AZX-703

Themes To Grow On
Fall & Winter

Table Of Contents

Managing Editor: Susan Walker

Editor at Large: Diane Badden

Contributing Writers: Bonnie Cave, Judy Huskins, Sandy McNeil

Copy Editors: Tazmen Carlisle, Karen Brewer Grossman, Amy Kirtley-Hill, Karen L. Mayworth, Kristy Parton, Debbie Shoffner, Cathy Edwards Simrell

Cover Artist: Nick Greenwood, Ivy L. Koonce

Artists: Jennifer Tipton Bennett, Cathy S. Bruce, Susan Hodnett, Donna K. Teal

The Mailbox® Books.com: Jennifer Tipton Bennett (DESIGNER/ARTIST); Stuart Smith (PRODUCTION ARTIST); Karen White (INTERNET COORDINATOR); Paul Fleetwood, Xiaoyun Wu (SYSTEMS)

President, The Mailbox Book Company™: Joseph C. Bucci

Director of Book Planning and Development: Chris Poindexter

Book Development Managers: Cayce Guiliano, Elizabeth H. Lindsay, Thad McLaurin

Editorial Planning: Kimberley Bruck (MANAGER); Debra Liverman, Sharon Murphy, Susan Walker (TEAM LEADERS)

Editorial and Freelance Management: Karen A. Brudnak; Hope Rodgers (EDITORIAL ASSISTANT)

Editorial Production: Lisa K. Pitts (TRAFFIC MANAGER); Lynette Dickerson (TYPE SYSTEMS); Mark Rainey (TYPESETTER)

Librarian: Dorothy C. McKinney

©2003 by THE EDUCATION CENTER, INC.
All rights reserved.
ISBN #1-56234-554-0

Except as provided for herein, no part of this publication may be reproduced or transmitted in any form or by any means, electronic or mechanical, including photocopying, recording, or storing in any information storage and retrieval system or electronic online bulletin board, without prior written permission from The Education Center, Inc. Permission is given to the original purchaser to reproduce patterns and reproducibles for individual classroom use only and not for resale or distribution. Reproduction for an entire school or school system is prohibited. Please direct written inquiries to The Education Center, Inc., P.O. Box 9753, Greensboro, NC 27429-0753. The Education Center®, *The Mailbox*®, the mailbox/post/grass logo, and The Mailbox Book Company™ are trademarks of The Education Center, Inc., and may be the subject of one or more federal trademark registrations. All other brand or product names are trademarks or registered trademarks of their respective companies.

Manufactured in the United States
10 9 8 7 6 5 4 3 2 1

Positional Words

Have several students stand in front of the room. Give each youngster a verbal direction telling where to stand in relationship to the other students. Use positional words such as *beside, in front of,* or *between* to position the students. For example, "Donna, stand *beside* Jamie." To vary this activity, have the seated students give the children the verbal directions using positional words.

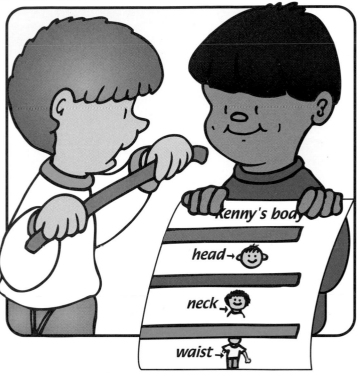

Measuring Up!

Organize children in groups of four. Give each child five strips of different-colored construction paper. Have each child use a different-colored paper strip to measure each part of his body. First have each child use a paper strip to measure around his head, cutting off the excess paper. Encourage each child to compare the length of his strip with those of the other children in the group. Glue each strip to a piece of personalized tagboard, making sure that the end of the strip is flush with the left-hand edge of the tagboard. Have the child label the strip by drawing the corresponding body part as shown. Repeat the same procedure for the neck, waist, wrist, and ankle.

Letter Counting And Sorting

Seat your youngsters around you. Encourage them to think of the first letter in their name. Hold up a flash card with a letter on it. Have each child whose name begins with that letter stand in a specific area of the room. Have one designated child in each group hold the letter flash card. Repeat these steps until all youngsters are standing in a group. Count the youngsters in each group and compare the total to the totals of the other groups. Invite your youngsters to determine which letter group has the most, the least, or the same amount.

LANGUAGE ARTS

The Howdy Hat

The Howdy Hat activity is an exciting way to introduce a variety of language skills and a rootin'-tootin' way to build self-esteem. To prepare for this activity, write each child's name on a strip of paper and place it in a cowboy hat. Keep a marker and several sheets of construction paper on hand (for a later activity). Pick one child's name from the hat. This will be your Howdy Hat child. Have youngsters ask questions to find out whose name was chosen from the hat. Encourage the youngsters to question such things as hair color, clothes the child is wearing, or the color of the child's eyes. Once the students have enough clues, have them guess the name of the Howdy Hat child. (Allow more questions if the guess is incorrect). If the guess is correct, the Howdy Hat child should come to the front of the room.

Next use the marker to write the Howdy Hat child's name on construction-paper sheets, printing one letter per sheet of construction paper. Have your students say the letters in her name. Count the letters in the child's name. Choose as many student volunteers as there are letters in the Howdy Hat child's name. Give each of them one of the letter cards. For example, if the child's name has five letters in it, then choose five student volunteers to hold the letters.

Now it's time to lead your students in a cheer for the Howdy Hat child! One at a time, have the student volunteers hold up the corresponding letters as you call out the letters in the Howdy Hat child's name. For example, if the child's name is Donna, say, "Give me a *D*." The class would then respond, "*D*." Continue cheering each letter in the child's name. Finally say, "What does that spell?" and the class will respond, "Donna."

End the activity by encouraging your students to tell the Howdy Hat child what they like about her, keeping the comments very positive. Continue this activity each day until every child's name has been drawn.

The Name Game

Have the children sit in a circle on the floor. Hold up a beanbag and say, "My name is _____, and I like _____." Pass the beanbag to the child beside you and have him repeat the sentence, inserting his name and the thing he likes. Continue around the circle until everyone has had a turn. Then go around the circle again and have student volunteers try to retell each child's name and the specific thing he likes.

Interest Inventory

Type an interest inventory similar to the one below. Send a copy home with each child. Ask him to return the completed copy the next day. Collect all of the inventories and read each one to the class, omitting the name of the child. Then ask the children to guess which classmate is being described.

All About Me

Parents, please help your child answer the following questions:

1. My name is _____.
2. I live at _____.
3. My phone number is _____.
4. My pets are _____.
5. These are the things I like to do: _____
   _____.
6. My favorite food is _____.
7. My favorite color is _____.
8. My favorite song is _____.
9. My favorite television show is _____
   _____.
10. When I grow up, I want to be _____
    _____.

Handful Of Fun!

Have each youngster trace one of his hands on construction paper. Then have him cut out the handprint. Encourage each child to think of two facts or interesting things about himself. Have him write or dictate for you to write these two things, printing one on the front and one on the back of the handprint. Have youngsters illustrate their sentences. These "handmade" creations are great for sharing!

Hello, my name is Caroline.

Can you find me?

Smile For The Camera

Take a picture of each child in the classroom individually and then in a group setting. Glue both pictures on a sheet of construction paper. Below the individual picture, print the sentence "Hello, my name is _____." Have each child fill in his name in the appropriate space. Below the group picture, print the sentence "Can you find me?" Then bind the papers together to create a class book. When the book is complete, share it with the students.

I love flowers.

I have a dog.

I am 5 years old.

I like to read.

Five-Star General

Make a class chart with five spaces beside each child's name. Tell the children that for each of the following tasks they complete, they will receive a red star beside their names on the chart:

Name five classmates.
Name the teacher.
Name the principal.
Name the school.
Know your first name, last name, and phone number.

When a child completes all five tasks, place a gold star on his forehead and send home a note or certificate describing his accomplishments. Vary and increase the difficulty of the tasks as the year progresses.

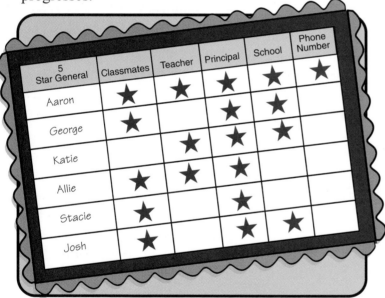

5 Star General	Classmates	Teacher	Principal	School	Phone Number
Aaron	★	★	★	★	★
George	★		★	★	
Katie		★	★	★	
Allie	★	★	★		
Stacie	★			★	
Josh	★			★	★

Language Experience

Read aloud *Things I Like* by Anthony Browne. Have students discuss the things that the monkey liked and why. Then have each child think of one thing that she likes and have her complete the sentence, "I like _____." Write each sentence on chart paper as it is dictated. Once all of the sentences have been recorded, copy each sentence on a separate sheet of paper. Give each child her sheet of paper and let her illustrate her sentence. Bind the papers together between construction-paper covers to make a class book. Title the cover of the book "Things We Like!"

SCIENCE

Time Capsule

Supply each child with an empty Pringles can and a large piece of construction paper. Have each child decorate the construction paper and glue it to the can to create a time capsule. Then encourage each child to fill his capsule with personal items such as a picture of himself, an example of his handwriting, and a drawing. Replace the plastic lids and store the time capsules until the end of the school year.

A Classroom Garden

To enhance a spirit of cooperation and develop a sense of community among your students, make a class garden. To make a class garden, select an area on the school grounds for a garden. Have each child plant a daffodil or tulip bulb. Throughout the school year, assist youngsters in maintaining the garden.

To vary this activity, adopt a class tree already on school grounds. The youngsters can name the tree, make bird feeders for it, use its leaves for various classroom projects, and observe and record the tree's changes each season.

Mrs. Bell's Class Garden

SOCIAL STUDIES

Faculty/Staff Introduction

Each day of the Getting To Know You unit, invite a faculty or staff member to spend time with your class. You may wish to invite the principal, school secretary, nurse, lunchroom personnel, or custodian. Encourage each guest to be prepared to talk to the class about his job responsibilities and to answer the youngsters' questions.

Class Video

Enlist the help of a fellow teacher or an older child in the school to videotape your class during one of the first weeks of school. Have the volunteer videotape a portion of each of the daily activities in which the class is involved. Make a special decorated bag for the video. Then send it home with a child each night until everyone has had a turn.

Class Directory

List each child's name in alphabetical order on a sheet of paper. Beside each name, list the child's address and phone number. Bind the list inside laminated covers to create a class directory. When a child needs a classmate's address or phone number, let him copy it from the book.

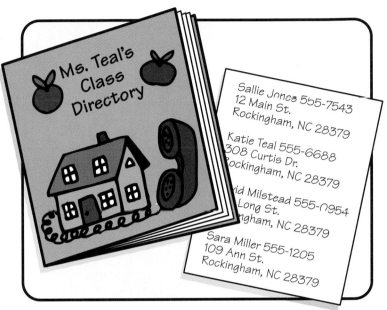

Ms. Teal's Class Directory

Sallie Jones 555-7543
12 Main St.
Rockingham, NC 28379

Katie Teal 555-6688
308 Curtis Dr.
Rockingham, NC 28379

David Milstead 555-0954
Long St.
ingham, NC 28379

Sara Miller 555-1205
109 Ann St.
Rockingham, NC 28379

Me Booklet

Thrill your little ones with this booklet that is big on self-esteem. Reproduce page 12 on white construction paper for each child. Have children color and illustrate each page and then cut on the bold lines. Stack the pages, use a hole punch where indicated, and tie the pages together with yarn. Provide time for your youngsters to share the contents of their books.

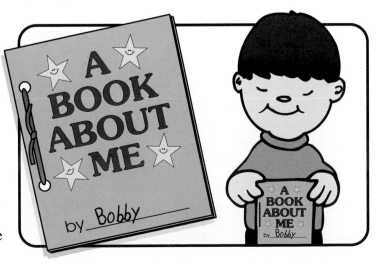

A BOOK ABOUT ME
by Bobby

ART

Self Collage

Tape a piece of paper to the wall. Place a lamp or over-head projector in front of the paper so that the light shines on it. In a learning center, have a child sit side-ways in the light of the lamp. Trace the child's silhouette onto the paper. Cut out the silhouette. Have the young-ster look through old magazines and cut out pictures of things that he likes. Students should then glue the maga-zine pictures in their silhouettes as collages. Please note that you may wish to have a teaching assistant or parent volunteer help you trace the silhouettes.

Friendship Sheet

Bring in a white, full-size sheet. Using a permanent marker, draw one large oval for each child around the perimeter of the sheet. Spread the sheet out on the floor. Have each child use bright-colored fabric paints to paint his face in one of the ovals. Once the fabric is dry, write the teacher's name, grade level, and room number in the center of the sheet. Then let the young-sters use fabric paint to make handprints on the sheet between their faces and the printing. This friendship sheet makes a great display in any classroom.

Bulletin Board

Display the many patches of friendship in your class-room by making this friendship quilt. To make a quilt, cut several squares of brightly colored construction paper. Give each child one of the squares. Have him glue a photograph of himself in the middle of the square. Have each child decorate the remainder of the square with yarn, beads, sequins, and glitter. Finally staple the squares, side by side, to the bulletin board to create a paper quilt. If extra squares are needed to fill the bulletin board, print information such as the school name or teacher's name on additional squares, and intermingle them with the students' squares as you staple them to the bulletin board.

Class Flip Book

Reproduce the paper doll outline on page 13 for each child. Have each child color the paper doll to resem-ble himself. Cut out the page on the top and bottom solid lines. Laminate each paper for durability. Bind the papers together to make a class book (spiral bind-ing is best for this activity). Cut each page apart on the two solid lines. Encourage the youngsters to ex-periment by flipping the top, middle, and bottom sections of the book to create different combinations of people.

SNACK

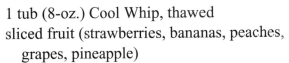

Fruity Friendship Pizza

1 package slice-and-bake sugar cookies

1 package (8-oz.) cream cheese, softened

1 tub (8-oz.) Cool Whip, thawed

sliced fruit (strawberries, bananas, peaches, grapes, pineapple)

Press the cookie dough into the bottom of a pizza pan. Bake it at 350° for 10 minutes. Blend the cream cheese and Cool Whip. Spread the mixture over the cooled cookie crust. Add the fruit. Pour on the Orange Sauce (below).

Orange Sauce

Stir together the following ingredients:

1/2 cup sugar

dash of salt

1 tablespoon cornstarch

Gradually add these ingredients to the mixture:

1/2 cup orange juice

2 tablespoons lemon juice

1/4 cup water

Cook the mixture until it thickens. Boil it for one minute. Pour it over the fruit. Slice and serve the fruit pizza.

CULMINATING ACTIVITY

Person To Person

Divide the class into pairs. Have partners face each other. Then name body parts that the partners must bring together. For example, you may call out, "Elbow to elbow," "Knees to knees," "Back to back," etc. Next call out, "Person to person," have everyone change partners, and begin the game again.

☆ A ☆
BOOK
ABOUT
☆ ME ☆

by _____

This is me!

This is where I live.

This is my family.

Teddy Bears

Every child loves teddy bears and bringing that special friend to school can be great fun! Using their own teddies is a "bear-y" nice way to get children involved in lots of fun-filled activities.

Opening Activity

On the first day of the Teddy Bears unit, send a note home with each child requesting that he bring a teddy bear to school the following day. Explain that the bears will be used throughout the week with several learning activities.

MATH

Circles Of Bears

Using three long pieces of yarn, make three large circles on the classroom floor. Tell children that they will sort their teddy bears to make sets of large, medium, and small bears. Then have the children place their bears in the circles according to size. Count and compare the number of bears in each set.

Pots Of Honey

Duplicate several copies of the bear and honey pot patterns on page 22. Cut out the patterns on the dotted lines. Place one bear and one honey pot on an overhead projector screen. Draw a line from the bear to the honey pot to demonstrate one-to-one correspondence. Then place various combinations of bears and honey pots on the overhead screen. Have volunteers draw lines between the bears and honey pots to show one-to-one correspondence.

Bear Patterning

Give each child in a learning center a small container of Gummy bears, crayons, and a copy of the bears worksheet on page 22. Have each child create an original color pattern using the Gummy bears. Then let him color the bears on the worksheet to represent the pattern of Gummy bears.

Positions

Use the patterns on page 22 to make nine bears of different colors and five honey pots of any color. Laminate them for durability. Then attach a strip of magnetic tape to the back of each bear and honey pot. Draw a large tic-tac-toe grid on a magnetic board. Place one bear in each of the nine squares. Use the board and the bears to review colors and positional words. For example, ask children to name the color of each bear on the board. Then have the youngsters use words such as *top*, *middle*, *bottom*, *left*, and *right* to describe each bear's position. Check your youngsters' understanding of the positions by first removing one of the bears from the grid. Then ask the youngsters to describe the position of the square from which the bear was taken. Repeat this procedure until the positions of all of the squares have been described.

Finally have the youngsters play a game of tic-tac-toe. Remove all of the bears from the magnetic board. Divide the youngsters into two groups. Give one group five bears as game pieces. Give the other group five honey pots as its game pieces. Have a child from one group bring a game piece to the board. Have the remaining members of his team describe the position of the square in which the game piece should be placed. Have the child place the game piece in that square. Then let the other group take a turn. Repeat until one group wins.

Sizing Up Teddies

Have your youngsters line up the teddy bears by size, starting with the smallest bear and ending with the biggest bear.

LANGUAGE ARTS

About My Bear

Have each child think of one thing that he can tell about his bear. Then have him complete the sentence, "My bear is _____." Write each sentence on chart paper as it is dictated. Then copy each sentence on a separate sheet of paper. Have each child illustrate his sentence. Bind the papers together between construction-paper covers to make a class book entitled "Our 'Bear-y' Special Friends."

Bear Hunt Timeline

Attach a large strip of paper to a chalkboard or wall. Give each child a strip of paper and crayons. Read the story *We're Going On A Bear Hunt* by Michael Rosen. As you read, draw a symbol for each of the places—such as the grass, river, mud, forest, mountains, snowstorm, and cave—through which the family must pass to find the bear. Have the children draw similar symbols on their papers. When you have finished the story, turn the timeline drawing over to the blank side of the paper, and reattach it to the chalkboard or wall. Instruct your students to turn over their drawings. Then have them recall the sequence of settings described in the story. As the youngsters recount the series of settings, draw each symbol on the blank side of the large strip of paper. Then have the youngsters turn their papers over and check the new timeline for accuracy.

Picnic Basket Goodies

Make a large picnic basket cutout from poster board. Attach the cutout to a chalkboard or wall. Lead the youngsters in singing Raffi's "Going On A Picnic" (from *The Corner Grocery Store And Other Singable Songs* cassette). Lead a class discussion to brainstorm all of the items mentioned in the song. Encourage the youngsters to think of other things that might be included in a picnic lunch. Have each child look through an old magazine and cut out one thing that he could take on a picnic. Glue the magazine pictures to the picnic basket cutout. Then lead the class in singing a new version of "Going On A Picnic." For example, point to a picture of brownies and sing, "Did you bring the brownies?" Have the class respond by singing, "Yes, we brought the brownies." Continue until you have included all of the children's picnic items in your song.

Teddy Bears

Following Directions

Tape a large piece of paper to the chalkboard or wall. Give each child a piece of paper and a pencil. Tell your children that they will follow your directions and will draw a teddy bear. Instruct them to listen carefully and draw each part of the bear after you demonstrate each step. While you draw give the following directions:

1. Draw one large circle in the center of your paper for the bear's body.
2. Draw a smaller circle on top of the body to make the bear's head.
3. Draw an arm on both sides of the body.
4. Draw two legs on the bottom of the body.
5. Draw two ears on the top of the bear's head.
6. Draw two eyes on the head.
7. Draw a nose below the eyes.
8. Draw a mouth below the nose.

SCIENCE

Bear Facts

Share factual information with your students using large, realistic pictures and the book *Bears, Bears And More Bears* by Jackie Morris. Then check recall of the information by using questions similar to those listed below. Have your youngsters put their thumbs up for a yes answer and thumbs down for no.

1. Bears come in many colors. *(Yes, black, brown, and white.)*
2. Most bears climb trees. *(Yes.)*
3. Most bears hibernate in the winter. *(Yes.)*
4. Most bears swim and run. *(Yes.)*
5. Bears eat candy. *(No. They eat berries, nuts, insects, fish, and small animals.)*

Hibernation

Read *Sleepy Bear* by Lydia Dabcovich. Discuss hibernation and other animals that hibernate such as groundhogs, frogs, and snakes.

SOCIAL STUDIES

Maps

Cut out or draw pictures of different kinds of bears such as brown, black, grizzly, or polar. Attach a large map of the world to a chalkboard or wall. Assemble your youngsters around the map. Discuss the habitats of the various bears. Then attach the bear pictures to the map to show where they can be found.

Teddy Bear Beginnings

Tell children the following story of the first teddy bears in the United States:

In 1902, President Theodore Roosevelt refused to shoot a helpless bear while on a hunting expedition. Many newspapers carried articles and cartoons about the president's act of kindness, and soon everyone knew about the event. In New York, a shopkeeper and his wife made two stuffed bears and displayed them in their shop window. The shopkeeper asked permission to call the toys Teddy's Bears in honor of the president. The stuffed bears were an instant success and since that time teddy bears have been a favorite toy of children all around the world.

Class Rules

Use bear puppets to reinforce class rules. Reproduce two bear patterns on page 22 for each child. To make bear puppets, have each child color both bears and cut around the solid dark line around the bear. Draw a smile on one bear and a frown on the other. Glue the two bears together back-to-back and attach them to a tongue depressor to create a puppet. Tell the youngsters that the happy bear's name is Behaving Bear, and it represents good behavior. The sad bear's name is Misbehaving Bear, and it represents unfavorable behavior. Describe various situations that could happen in the classroom. When a situation is described where class rules are being followed, children should hold up Behaving Bear. When a situation is described where class rules are being broken, children should hold up Misbehaving Bear.

ART

Bear Painting

In a small group, ask each child to think of his favorite bear. Then give him a large piece of white construction paper. To make a bear painting, have each child use a crayon to draw the face of the bear on the paper. Draw the appropriate foliage around the bear such as leaves, trees, vines, or grass. Paint the picture using tempera paints. Allow the paint to dry. Then have your youngsters use black tempera paint or another dark color to outline the bear and foliage.

Bear Faces

Supply each child in a small group with a copy of the bear face worksheet on page 23. Supply each group with paper towels and containers of dark brown, light brown, and black paint. To make a bear face, have each child draw a mouth on the bear with a crayon. Then tell each child to dip his index finger in the dark brown paint. Have him fill in the ears and head surrounding the snout with small circular motions. Next have him dip his finger into the light brown paint and fill in the insides of the snout and ears. Finally have him dip his finger in the black paint and create the eyes, nose, and mouth of the bear. **Please note:** children should wipe off their fingers with paper towels before changing paint colors.

A "Bear-y" Big Collage

Have your youngsters look for pictures of bears in old magazines, storybooks, and science magazines. Have them cut out the bear pictures. Paste the pictures on a large bear cutout made from tagboard.

Clay Creatures

Lead a class discussion about the physical attributes of a bear. Include topics such as how many legs a bear has, if it has a tail, and what its face looks like. Then supply each child with a ball of clay and encourage children to make bears. Place all of the clay bears on a table in a center. Allow children to make trees and grass from construction and tissue paper to add to the clay bear collection.

Circle Bears

Make several large, medium, and small circle patterns using cardboard. Have each child in a small group trace and cut out two large circles, two medium circles, and six small circles from construction paper. Give each child a large piece of construction paper. Have him glue the large circles on the paper to form the head and body of the bear. Then glue the medium circles onto the large circles to make the bear's stomach and snout. Finally have him glue the small circles on the bear body to make the legs, arms, and ears. Draw the eyes and nose on the bear using a marker or crayon.

Stuffed Bears

Have your youngsters make "bear-y" cute stuffed teddies to take home. Have each child cut two identical bear shapes from craft paper and then decorate them. Staple halfway around the edge of the bear shapes. Stuff the bear with newspaper; then staple the other half of the bear shapes together.

SNACK

Jamberry Treat

1 tablespoon sour cream
1/4 teaspoon brown sugar
2 heaping teaspoons of berries (any
   combination of blackberries, blueberries,
   and/or raspberries)

Have each child prepare his own individual treat. Set the ingredients and measuring spoons on a table. Then give each child a three-ounce paper cup and a plastic spoon. Let him measure the ingredients, mix them together, and eat the treat.

CULMINATING ACTIVITY

A Teddy Bear Picnic

This activity was designed to help familiarize children with the school building and school personnel. On the last day of the unit, read *The Teddy Bears' Picnic* by Jimmy Kennedy. Show the children a picnic basket full of things that teddy bears might pack for a picnic lunch such as honey sandwiches, Teddy Grahams, Gummy Bears, and juice. Place the picnic basket on the floor and have children put their teddy bears around it. Take the class out of the room for a break. Have a teacher or parent secretly take the lunch and the teddy bears to a predetermined place and set up the picnic on picnic blankets. When the youngsters return, tell them that the teddy bears and basket have disappeared. Lead the class in finding the missing bears and basket. This part of the activity must be discussed with key faculty members prior to the search for the teddy bears. Inform faculty members to tell your class that they saw the teddy bears going down the hall to a specific location. For example, take the children to the principal's office. Ask the principal if he has seen a group of teddy bears going down the hall with a picnic basket. The principal will tell the class that he just saw them running past his office in the direction of the library. Continue the search throughout the school building until you finally arrive at the predetermined picnic location; then enjoy!

Teddy Bears   Use with "Bear Patterning" on page 14.

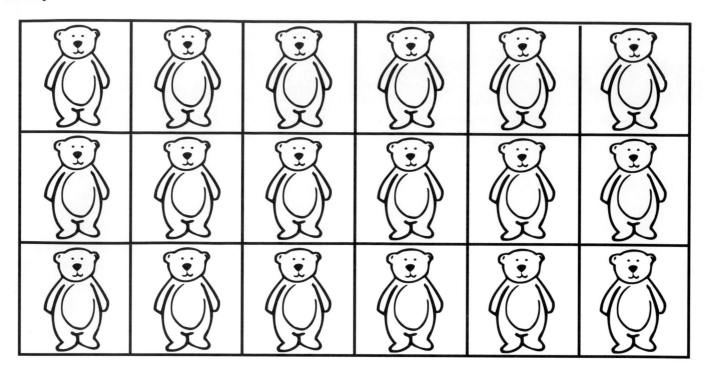

©The Education Center, Inc. • *Themes to Grow On* • *Fall & Winter* • TEC60799

Patterns

Use with "Pots Of Honey" on page 14, "Positions" on page 15, and "Class Rules" on page 18.

HONEY POT

©The Education Center, Inc. • *Themes to Grow On* • *Fall & Winter* • TEC60799

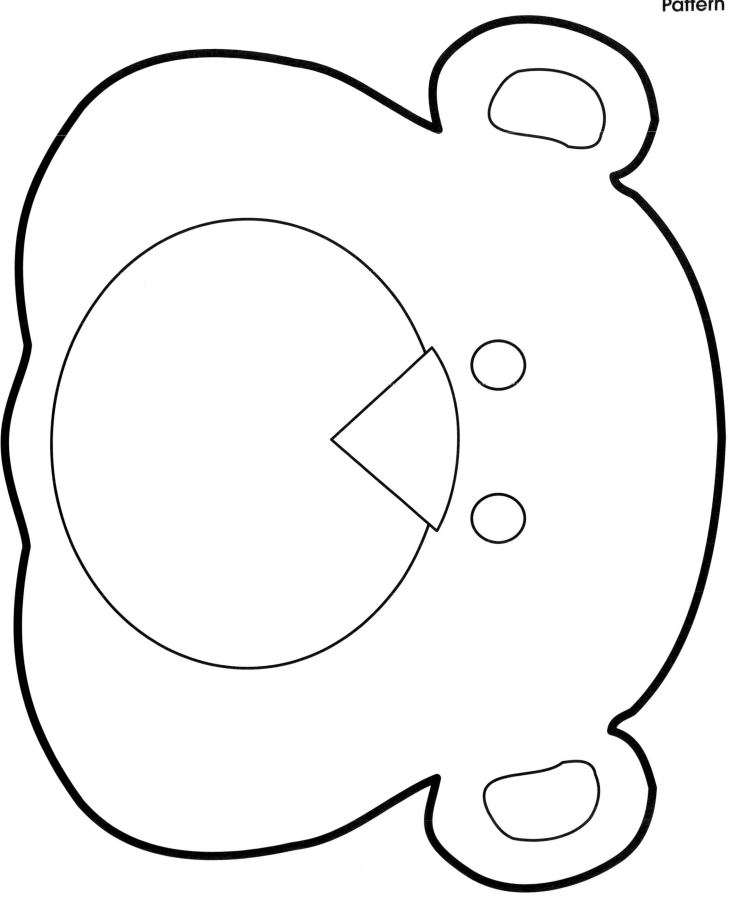

Birthday Celebrations With Clifford

Birthdays are special days. Celebrate by learning about each other's birthdays while having fun with the lovable dog Clifford.

Opening Activity

Plan a week of activities around Clifford. Begin by duplicating Clifford's paw print on page 32 on red construction paper. The day before the unit is to begin, attach several paw prints to the floor using clear Con-Tact paper or masking tape. To spark children's interest, make a trail of the paw prints beginning in the hallway and leading into the classroom.

MATH

Graphing Birthdays

Make a large graph with a list of all of the months of the year on the left-hand side of the graph. Post the graph in the classroom so it is visible to each child. Review the months of the year and indicate whose birthday comes in each month. Give each child a red paw print (page 32) with his name and birth date printed on it. Then call out the months of the year, one at a time. Have the students come up to the graph when their birthday month is named and attach their paw prints in the appropriate row. Finally have the youngsters decide which month has the most/least birthdays.

Graphing

Provide a bowl with several colored dog biscuits in it for each child. Give each child in a small group one of the bowls, crayons, and a copy of the graph on page 33. Have each youngster sort out one color of dog biscuit. Have him graph the results by coloring in the squares. Have children compare their results to see who had the most/least biscuits of each color.

Sorting

Provide a small group of youngsters with a large box of candles that vary in sizes, colors, and shapes. Have the students decide how they will classify the candles. Encourage them to think about the sizes, textures, colors, and shapes of the candles. Then let the group sort the candles accordingly.

Counting Math Book

Create a "Paw Prints Math Book" for each child in the class. Staple blank sheets of paper inside a folded piece of construction paper. Number the pages from one to ten as shown. Supply each child in a learning center with one of these books, a stamp pad, and a paw print stamp. (Provide red crayons if a paw print stamp is not available.) Have the youngsters look at the numerals printed on the pages and stamp (or draw with red crayons) the corresponding number of paws on each page.

Biscuit Counting

Review number identification and counting skills with this nifty idea. Number ten paper plates from one to ten by writing a numeral in the center of each plate. Place the plates in a learning center with a container of 55 small dog biscuits. Have the children identify the numerals on the plates and place the appropriate number of dog biscuits on them.

Where's The Bone?

Supply each child with a dog biscuit. Have the children listen as you direct them to place the biscuits in various positions. For example, tell the children to put their dog biscuits under their chairs, between their knees, or on top of their heads.

LANGUAGE ARTS

Letter Recognition

In a small group, have your youngsters use red clay and a set of alphabet cookie cutters to make the letters of the alphabet or the letters in their names.

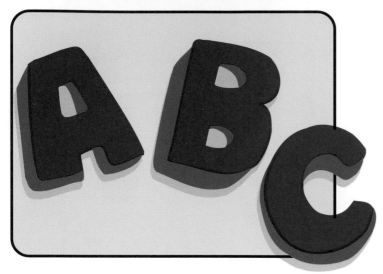

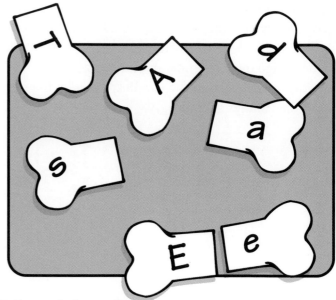

Letter/Sound Recognition

Reproduce 26 bones from page 32 on construction paper. Print each letter of the alphabet on an individual bone and laminate them. Cut out the bones. Place each bone atop an object that begins with the corresponding letter. Allow each child an opportunity to find at least one bone. Have him name the letter on the bone, make its sound, and tell the name of the object that begins with that sound. On the following day, give one bone cutout to each child in the class and have him place it on an object in the room that begins with that sound.

Matching Bones

Duplicate the bone pattern on page 32 on construction paper to make 26 bones. On one half of each bone, write an uppercase letter and on the other half, write the corresponding lowercase letter. Laminate the bones, cut them out, and then cut them in half. Place all of the bone sections in a learning center and have the students put them back together by matching the upper- and lowercase letters.

A variation of this activity is to make a set of bones that each have a letter on one half and a picture of something that begins with that letter on the other half. Youngsters match each picture with the letter representing its beginning sound. You can color code the back of each half for self-checking.

Reading About Clifford

Norman Bridwell has written over 30 Clifford books. During this unit introduce your class to Clifford by reading *Clifford the Small Red Puppy*, *Clifford The Big Red Dog,* and *Clifford's Birthday Party*. Set up a table in the room to display some of the many other Clifford titles. Youngsters can choose a Clifford book to review or read.

Birthday Gifts

In preparation for Clifford's birthday party (see the Culminating Activity on page 31), have your youngsters think of a gift that they would like to give Clifford. Then have them complete the sentence, "I will give Clifford _____." Write each child's sentence on chart paper as she dictates it. Once everyone has dictated a sentence, copy the sentences on individual sheets of paper, roll each sheet, write each child's name on the back of his paper, and tie a piece of ribbon around each one. Then place all of the rolls in a basket. On the day of the party, have each child unroll her sheet of paper and read aloud what she would give Clifford on his birthday.

Red Things

Clifford is a big red dog. Ask a group of children to name things that are red. As they call out the names of red things, list them on chart paper using a red marker. After each word is printed, allow the child who thought of the word an opportunity to read it. Then cut out the words. Give each child his word and a piece of paper with the sentence, "A _____ is red," printed at the bottom. Read the sentence to the students and have each of them complete it by copying his word in the blank. Assist those students who have difficulty with copying. Have the students illustrate their sentences. Bind the papers together to make a class book. Title the book "What Is Red?"

SCIENCE

A "Sound" Idea For Science

Put a different object into each of five small boxes. Wrap the boxes to resemble birthday presents. Number the presents from one to five and place them in a learning center. Have children gently shake each box, listen to the sound, and guess what is inside. Then give each child a blank piece of paper and have him number it from one to five. Have each child draw a picture of the object that he thinks is in each box beside the appropriate number on his paper. (Most youngsters will need to listen to the sounds made by the objects more than once before deciding what to draw.) Have the children discuss what the guesses were. Then open the boxes to show what's inside!

"Feely" Box

Cover a large box and its lid separately with birthday wrapping paper. Cut a hole in the lid that is large enough for a child to insert her hand. Place several things a dog might use inside the box, such as a dog dish, ball, brush, collar, bone, or leash. Put the lid on the box and attach a bow to the lid so the hole is not covered. In a small group, have each youngster reach into the box, pick up one object, describe how it feels, and guess the name of the object. When each child has had at least one turn, open the box and take out its contents.

28

SOCIAL STUDIES

Community Helpers

Ask a veterinarian or a member of the Humane Society to come to your class and talk about how his or her work helps dogs. Also ask your guest to be prepared to discuss how dogs should be cared for by their owners.

Famous Dogs

Talk about famous dogs such as Lassie or Benji. Encourage children to bring in books or articles about or pictures of famous dogs that can be shared with the class.

Dog Helpers

Discuss ways in which dogs help people. Then follow up the discussion by reading a book such as *Books For Young Explorers (Set 1): Dogs Working For People* by Joanna Foster.

Where Were You Born?

Write the name of each child and the state in which he was born on a slip of paper (you can find the name of the state in each child's office records). Then attach a large map of the United States to a bulletin board or corkboard. Give each child her slip of paper. Call out the name of each state and have children stand up when their state is named. For each child who was born in a particular state, add a straight pin to the map. Then count the number of pins inserted into each state. Finally make a list of the states, beginning with the state in which the most children were born and ending with the state in which the fewest were born.

ART

Clifford Ears

Cut a 1" x 25" strip of tagboard for each child in the classroom. Make a headband for each child by first wrapping the strip around his head and cutting off the excess paper. Then write the word "Clifford" on the tagboard strip and staple the ends together. Next give each child two pieces of red construction paper. Have him cut out two large ears. Staple the ears to the tagboard strip. Encourage each child to wear his Clifford ears while the class sings "Do Your Ears Hang Low?"

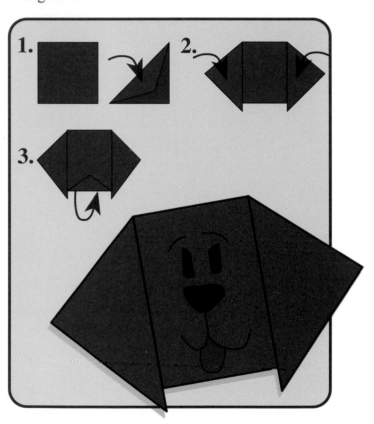

Party Decorations

Have your youngsters make the decorations for Clifford's birthday party celebration (see the Culminating Activity on page 31). Have each child decorate his own placemat, napkin, plate, and cup for the party. Also have the students make paper garlands and a poster that says, "Happy Birthday, Clifford."

Origami

Give each child a nine-inch square of red construction paper. Have him fold the paper in half to form a triangle (Step 1). Then have him fold the top two corners down in front (Step 2) and the bottom corner up in back (Step 3). Turn the paper over. Have him use a black marker or crayon to draw a dog's face in the center. Finally tape a drinking straw to the back to make a Clifford puppet.

Birthday Banners

Have all of the youngsters who have birthdays in the same month work together in a center to create a birthday banner. First place a large sheet of paper in the learning center. Then have your youngsters plan how they will transform the paper into an attractive banner. They may wish to include self-portraits, examples of their best work, a calendar, or some seasonal pictures that reflect this month of the year. After the banners are completed, store them. Take out the appropriate banner for each month and display it. Encourage the children whose birthdays fall in the summer months (or any months that you're not in school) to complete their banners, and display them before school is dismissed for summer vacation.

SNACK

Peanut Butter Bones

2 cups nonfat dry milk
2 cups peanut butter (or soy nut butter)
4 tablespoons honey
1/2 cup finely crushed graham-cracker crumbs

Mix together the dry milk and peanut butter.
Add the honey and stir well. Divide the mixture
into 24 individual balls. Give each child a ball.
Have him mold it into the shape of a bone.
Sprinkle each peanut-butter bone on both sides
with the graham-cracker crumbs.

CULMINATING ACTIVITY

Clifford's Birthday Party

Plan a birthday party for Clifford on the final day of
this unit. Begin by sending home an invitation to the
party with each child. The information on the invitation should include the day and time of the party,
instructions for each child to wear something red, and
a homework assignment to make an original party hat.
(The assignment must be completed by the day of the
party.)

On the day of the party, help the children put up the
decorations that they have made (see "Party Decorations" on page 30). Then have the children play
Doggie, Doggie, Who's Got The Bone? Serve cake
and red fruit punch, and as a party favor, give each
child a stick of Big Red chewing gum. Have each
child read aloud what she would give Clifford on his
birthday (see "Birthday Gifts" on page 27). The party
and the week of learning activities centered around
Clifford are guaranteed to be a hit!

Birthday Celebrations With Clifford
Patterns

Use with "Opening Activity" and "Graphing Birthdays" on page 24.

©The Education Center, Inc. • *Themes to Grow On* • *Fall & Winter* • TEC60799

Use with "Matching Bones" and "Letter/Sound Recognition" on page 26.

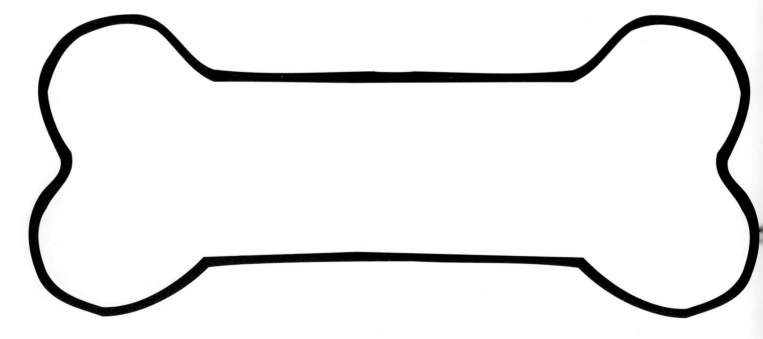

©The Education Center, Inc. • *Themes to Grow On* • *Fall & Winter* • TEC60799

Name _____

6				
5				
4				
3				
2				
1				

©The Education Center, Inc. • *Themes to Grow On • Fall & Winter* • TEC60799

Use with "Graphing" on page 24.

Pets

Most children have had experience with pets in their homes or in their neighborhoods. Giving children the opportunity to discuss, observe, and compare pets in the classroom will help them develop responsible attitudes towards other living things.

MATH

Pet Floor Graph

Have each child draw a picture of her pet on a 3" x 5" index card. Arrange the children in a semicircle on the floor with their pet cards. Hold up and read word cards with different pet names on them. As you read each pet name, ask each child who has a picture of that pet to place his picture card next to the pet word card as shown. Repeat this step until every child has placed his pet picture beside the matching pet word card. Then use the picture graph to compare the numbers of each type of pets owned by the children in the classroom.

Pet Patterning

Move the pet picture cards made by the children from the floor graph to a learning center. Encourage the youngsters in the center to use the cards to create original patterns.

Fishing For Numbers!

Give each child a copy of the fish/fishbowl worksheet on page 43. Have him cut out the fish on the dotted lines; then paste each fish on the corresponding fishbowl to match the numeral with the correct set.

Time Of Day

Create a time-of-day worksheet by using a marker to divide a piece of paper into four equal parts. Write one of the words *morning, noon, afternoon,* and *evening* at the top of each part respectively. Duplicate the worksheet for each child. For homework, ask each child to draw a picture of what her pet does during that particular time of day. Tell the children that they may need their parents' help with this activity.

Number Words

Write the numerals one, two, three, and four on the chalkboard. Under each numeral, write the corresponding number word. Encourage your youngsters to think of words that rhyme with each number word. Write the rhyming words under the number words. Then have each child choose a rhyming word for each number and draw a rhyming number/word picture for each pair. Bind the papers together to make individual books.

Pets And Sets

Use pet items brought in by students to create sets of four. In each set place three things that go together and one thing that does not belong. Ask youngsters to look at each of the sets. Have them distinguish which of the items belong together and which does not. Have them give rationales for their choices.

1	2	3	4	5
one	two	three	four	five
fun	shoe	knee	door	dive
sun	flew	bee	floor	live
bun	new	key	soar	

Stacie — Three Key

Kevin — one sun

Molly — two shoe

LANGUAGE ARTS

Pondering Pets

Read the book *Dear Zoo* by Rod Campbell. This book will help youngsters think of reasons why certain animals make better pets than others. After reading the book, have the children brainstorm the characteristics of a good pet. Then have them think of animals that would make suitable pets.

Pet Pals

After reading and discussing several books about pets, let each child tell about his pet. (Children who do not have pets may describe a pet that they would like to own.) Ask him to complete the sentence, "My pet is a _____." Write each sentence on chart paper as it is dictated and add each child's name beside his response. Copy the sentences on individual pieces of paper. Give each child the piece of paper with his sentence written at the bottom. Have him illustrate the sentence. Bind the papers together to create a class book.

Word Wheel

In a small group, lead the children in a discussion about pets. Have each group choose one pet. Write the name of this pet in the center of a large piece of paper. Draw a circle around the pet name. Ask the youngsters to think of words that could describe the pet. Draw lines from the circle outward and write a descriptive word at the end of each line. Repeat the procedure for other pets. Then have each child choose one of the pets and draw a picture to illustrate the words shown in the word wheel. Attach the pictures to the appropriate word wheel.

Sharing Pets

Obtain the permission of a few parents for their children to share their pets with the class. Schedule a specific time during each day of the pet unit for parents to bring the pets to school. Have the child who owns the pet describe its care, the food it eats, the type of exercise it requires, and where it is kept. Then allow the youngsters time to ask questions about the pet of the day.

Class Book

Read Eric Carle's *Have You Seen My Cat?* Then have your youngsters use the same format as the book to write a book entitled "Have You Seen My Pet?" Have one child draw an animal that would make a good pet. Write "This is my pet." below the drawing. Then have one child draw an animal that would not make a good pet. Write "This is not my pet." below that drawing. Continue in the same fashion. Bind the papers together to make a class book.

Rhyming Words

List the words *dog, cat, fish, bunny,* and *mouse* on the chalkboard. List words that rhyme with each of the pet names as your students dictate them. Then have your youngsters supply rhyming words to complete the following sentences:

I have a dog that jumps like a _____.
I have a cat that wears a red _____.
I have a fish that swims in a _____.
I have a bunny that looks very _____.
I have a mouse that lives in a _____.

dog	cat	fish	bunny	mouse
log	hat	dish	funny	house
clog	mat	wish	money	
frog	sat		sunny	
	fat			

SCIENCE

Class Pet

Adopt a class pet such as a hamster, gerbil, turtle, or fish that can remain in the classroom throughout the school year. Discuss the proper care of this pet with the class. Each week, assign a child the responsibility of feeding and caring for the pet.

Pets/Not Pets

Cut out several pictures of animals from magazines. Glue the pictures to a large piece of poster board. Laminate the poster for durability. Attach the poster to a wall or chalkboard. Have a volunteer come up to the poster. Have him use a grease pencil to either circle an animal that could be a pet or cross out an animal that could not. Continue until all of the animals are either circled or crossed out.

Thinking Exercise

Read the following sentences about pets and have your youngsters name each pet that you describe:

I am thinking of a pet that likes to drink milk and purrs when it is happy. *(cat)*

I am thinking of a pet that is green or brown and wears its house on its back. *(turtle)*

I am thinking of a pet that likes to eat carrots and has long ears. *(rabbit)*

I am thinking of a pet that has been called man's best friend. *(dog)*

I am thinking of a small pet that lives in a cage and sleeps during the day. *(gerbil or hamster)*

I am thinking of a pet that lives in a cage and squeals or whistles at mealtime. *(guinea pig)*

Pet Items

Encourage each child who owns a pet to bring in one pet item from home such as a leash, toy, or brush. Place the items in a large box. Take the items out of the box one by one. Have the students name the pet or pets with which each item could be used. Use these with "Pets And Sets" on page 35.

SOCIAL STUDIES

Pet Care

Invite a guest from the Animal Control Shelter or Humane Society to visit your class. These organizations will present programs designed to teach children about pet care, leash laws, and training. Other invited guests such as a veterinarian or kennel club member can describe their work with their animal friends.

Pet Needs

Reproduce the six cards on page 42. Color each of the pictures. Cut apart the cards on the solid lines. Attach each card to an index card. Laminate the cards for durability. Use the cards with children to discuss the basic needs of pets such as food, water, housing, grooming, exercise, and love. Discuss the various ways that these needs can be met by the owners of different kinds of pets.

Class Pet Store

After the field trip to the pet store, set up a pet store in the classroom. Place a toy cash register, play money, stuffed animals, and pet care items in the classroom pet store. Have small groups of children take turns pretending that they are the store attendants and customers.

Pet Store

Plan a field trip to a pet store. Ask the store attendant to describe the different types of pets and pet care items found in the store.

ART

Pet Masks

Have your youngsters create pet masks. To make a pet mask, give each child a paper plate. Have her paint one side of the plate with tempera paints. Allow the paint to dry. Decorate the plate with facial features by using paper scraps, yarn, and feathers. Cut the eyes out of the mask so that youngsters will be able to see. Glue a tongue depressor to the bottom of each plate for the handle. Have your youngsters participate in a pet parade by holding their pet masks in front of their faces and marching around the classroom.

Thumbprint Pets

Place a few stamp pads and a supply of paper in a learning center. Ask each child to create several thumbprints by pressing her thumb in a stamp pad and then pressing it on a sheet of the paper. Then have her use a fine-line marker to draw features on each of the thumbprints to create different pets.

Origami Puppets

Give each child in a small group a 9" x 12" piece of construction paper. Have him fold it in thirds, lengthwise (Step 1). Then fold it in quarters with the open ends touching in the middle (Step 2). Fold the paper in half so the open ends are on the outside. Then have him make pet features using paper scraps, pom-poms, and feathers. Glue them to the origami puppet (Step 3). Have the child slip his fingers in the top opening and thumb in the bottom opening to move the puppet's mouth.

Lacing Pets

Supply each child with a 9" x 12" piece of tagboard to make a laced pet. Have each child draw a pet on it. Paint the pet with tempera paint. When the paint is dry, cut out the pet painting. Use a hole puncher to punch holes around the perimeter of each pet (leaving at least a half-inch between each hole). Lace through the holes with a piece of yarn. Tie the ends together to secure the yarn in place.

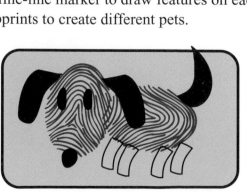

SNACK

CULMINATING ACTIVITY

Celebrate the conclusion of pet week with a pet show featuring class members and their pets. Arrange a time when parents can bring the pets to school. Pets suitable for a classroom setting may stay the entire day. Other pets should be scheduled to arrive at ten-minute intervals to avoid a number of pets being in the room at the same time. Encourage children without pets to draw or bring a picture of a pet that they would like to own.

Fruit Pets

Have each child create an original fruit pet. Give her a canned peach or pear half on a small paper plate. Then let her choose from a variety of foods to create the features. Toothpicks may be needed to attach some of the foods to the fruit.

1 canned peach or pear half for each child
1 small paper plate for each child
various foods for features, including:
    raisins
    miniature marshmallows
    carrot curls
    cloves
    cherries
    chocolate chips
    grapes
    gumdrops
    toothpicks

Use with "Pet Needs" on page 39.

©The Education Center, Inc. • *Themes to Grow On* • *Fall & Winter* • TEC60799

Name

Fishing For Numbers!

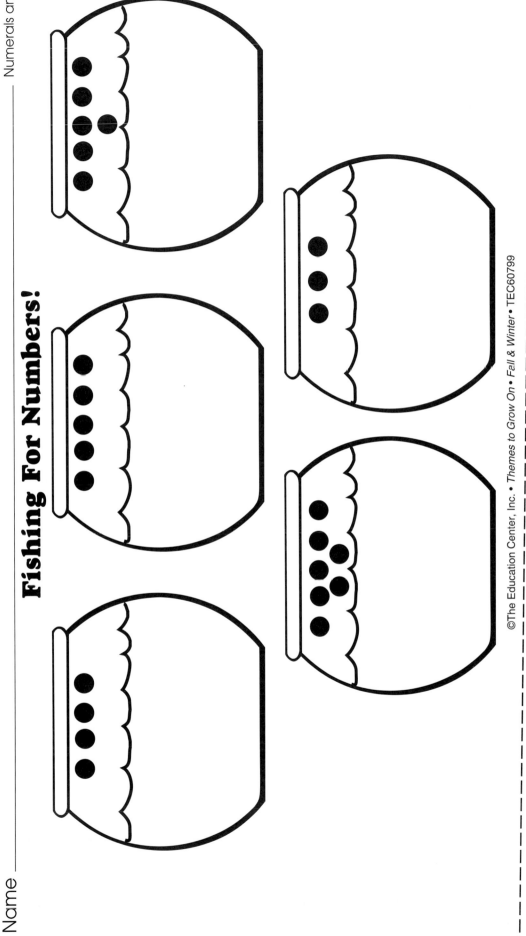

©The Education Center, Inc. • *Themes to Grow On • Fall & Winter* • TEC60799

Use with "Fishing For Numbers!" on page 34.

43

Colors And Shapes

Colors and shapes are part of a child's everyday experiences. These activities will heighten his awareness and understanding of the colors and shapes that fill his world.

MATH

Basket Of Shapes

Place a variety of plastic shapes in a basket. Cover a die on each of its six sides with pictures of the same shapes as those in the basket. (White self-sticking labels can be easily cut to fit over the sides of the die and then a shape can be drawn on each of the sides with a permanent marker.) Put the basket of shapes and the die in a learning center. Have each child roll the die, look at the shape that is pictured on the top of the die, and select a shape from the basket that is similar. Have youngsters continue to play until all of the shapes are gone from the basket. Then ask each child to sort and count her different shapes. Give her a sheet of paper. Have her draw a picture of each of the six shapes on the paper. Then ask her to make tally marks beside each of the shapes to show how many she has. Finally have the youngsters in the center compare their totals.

Parts To A Whole

Make several task cards picturing various building block structures. Have each child in a learning center select one of the cards. Encourage him to use building blocks to copy the model pictured on the task card. When the model has been completed, point out the different parts used to make the whole. Have the students exchange task cards and begin the activity again, or ask each child to build his own model and create a corresponding task card that may be used in the center.

Clay Boards

Draw several shapes on large strips of tagboard. Laminate the strips for durability. Have the young-sters use clay to form shapes over those drawn, letters, and sight words.

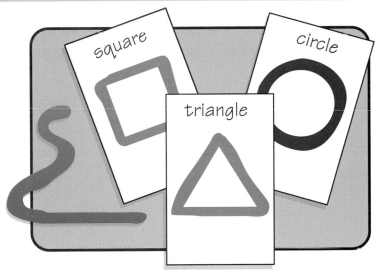

Shapes/Shape Words

Youngsters will enjoy putting these shape puzzles together in a math center. To make a shape word puzzle, cut cardboard into strips approximately 3" x 8" in size. Draw a shape on the left-hand side of each strip. Write the name for each shape on the right-hand side of the strip. Cut apart each strip between the shape and the printed word. (The same procedure can be used to make color word puzzles.) Place all of the puzzle pieces in a basket. To use the center, have youngsters put the puzzle pieces together by matching each shape to the shape word.

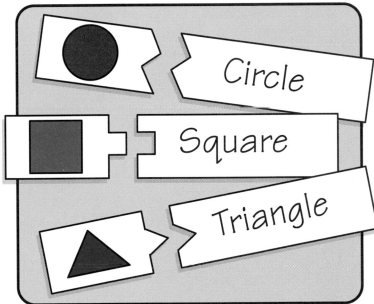

Twister

To review colors, have your youngsters play the game Twister.

LANGUAGE ARTS

Color Categories

Write each of the following color words and categories on chart paper using a marker of the same color. Have the youngsters name things that could be included in each of the categories listed beside the color words. Write the items mentioned by the students on the chart paper under the corresponding color word and catagory.

green—things outside
yellow—foods
red—vehicles
blue—clothes
brown—toys
black—animals
purple—things you would bring to school
orange—things in the classroom

Have each child make an individual color book by choosing one of the items from each of the lists and drawing a picture of it on a piece of paper. Write the color word and the item name below each drawing. Bind the papers together.

Color Sorting

Obtain several paint sample cards from a paint store. Cut apart the individual colors on each of the cards. Place the color cards in a basket. Have the students in a learning center sort the cards by color.

What's Missing?

Cut out several squares of different colors of construction paper and laminate them. Attach felt to the back of each square. Place four of the squares on a flannelboard. Have your youngsters observe the color of each of the four squares. Have youngsters close their eyes. Remove one of the squares. Ask them to open their eyes. Have the youngsters tell which color is missing. Repeat the activity using different squares.

Following Directions

Have your youngsters color the worksheet on page 52 by using the coloring key printed at the top of the page.

SCIENCE

Prism Rainbow

Show your students the correct order of the colors in a rainbow. Place a prism in front of a powerful light source such as a slide projector. Project the colors on a screen or a solid white surface. The colors will be bright and easy for the children to see.

- red
- orange
- yellow
- green
- blue
- violet

Color Mixing

Fill several empty baby food jars half full of water. Place the jars, several eyedroppers, and food coloring in a learning center. Have the youngsters in the center wear paint smocks. Instruct the students that the *primary colors* are red, blue, and yellow. Explain that they can make the other colors in the rainbow by using different combinations of these three colors. Supply each child with a jar of water and an eyedropper. Have her use the eyedropper to put yellow food coloring into the water. Tell her that she can make the water orange by adding some red food coloring. Then replace the water in their jars and guide your youngsters to make the colors purple and green.

Shape Walk Observation

Take a shape walk outside. Escort your youngsters outdoors and as you walk, have the children look for things made in the shapes of circles, squares, triangles, and rectangles. When someone sees a shape, have him raise his hand and when called on say, "I spy a shape." Ask the child what shape he sees. Allow him to answer and show the particular object that resembles the shape.

Magic Ice Experiment

For this activity you will need red, yellow, and blue food coloring; eyedroppers; salt; 1/4-cup measure; three bowls; water; pie tins; and blocks of ice. (To make the blocks of ice large enough for this experiment, freeze water in small cartons.)

To conduct the experiment, pour one-fourth cup of water into each of the three bowls. Add three drops of blue food coloring and a dash of salt to one of the bowls of water. Repeat this procedure using the red and yellow food coloring in the other two bowls. Then give each child in a learning center a pie tin with a block of ice in the middle. Have him use an eyedropper to put two or three drops of blue water on the top of his block of ice. Then have him add two or three drops of yellow water to the top of the ice. Have him observe as the colors penetrate the ice and mix to make a new color. Next have him put two or three drops of red water on the top of the ice. Encourage him to watch the ice and tell what new colors he sees as the red, yellow, and blue mix together inside the block of magic ice.

SOCIAL STUDIES

Cooperative-Learning Groups

Divide the class into four groups. Supply each group with multicolored construction paper, pencils, scissors, and various size patterns for each of the shapes to be traced. Assign each group a different shape to make. Have each child in a group trace and cut out the shapes using different colors of paper. Collect the shapes made by each group and place them in a basket. Then distribute the shapes among the four groups so that each group has some of each of the shapes (each group does not have to have the same number of different shapes). Encourage the youngsters in each group to work together and use their set of shapes to plan a shape picture. Have them glue their shape picture on a large sheet of paper. Allow each group time to share how they worked together to create the picture.

Shape Animals

Reproduce each of the shape animals found on page 53 on individual pieces of paper. Laminate the shape animals and put them in a learning center. To use the center, have each child choose one of the animal shapes and trace around it. Encourage the youngsters to add facial features and internal lines to finish the animal shapes.

ART

Torn Tissue Paper

Tear several sheets of bright-colored tissue paper into various size pieces. Place the torn tissue paper in a learning center. Give each child in the center a sheet of tagboard, a paintbrush, and a bowl of diluted glue. Give him the opportunity to choose several pieces of tissue paper and place them on his sheet of tagboard. (The pieces of tissue paper should overlap one another and cover the tagboard.) Have him use the paintbrush to paint the diluted glue over the surface of the paper. Allow time for the glue to dry and coat it with an acrylic polymer if a glossy sheen is desired.

Sun Catcher

Put those old crayon pieces to good use by making a colorful sun catcher. To make a sun catcher, grate some old crayons. Place the crayon shavings of like colors in separate containers. Give each child two squares of waxed paper. Have her sprinkle the crayon shavings on one piece of the waxed paper. Have her place the other waxed paper square on top of the shavings. Place the waxed paper squares on a towel and then place a cloth over the waxed paper. Iron over the waxed paper until the crayon shavings in the center are melted. (Ironing is to be done by the teacher.) Allow time for the waxed paper to cool. Glue four tongue depressors over the edges of the paper square to make a frame. Attach a piece of yarn to the back to suspend the sun catcher. Mount it in a sunny window and enjoy the beautiful colors!

Shape Art

Have your youngsters trace many different-sized circles on different colors of construction paper. Have them cut out the circles. Have them glue the bigger circles on a large piece of construction paper, filling the paper and touching all four edges of the paper. Glue the smaller circles inside the bigger circles. Allow them to continue this until all of the circles are filled with a number of smaller circles. Put these colorful circle collages on display. (To vary this activity, try using squares, triangles, or other shapes.)

A Colorful Bulletin Board

On art paper, have each youngster make red, orange, yellow, green, blue, and purple tempera-paint handprints. When the handprints are dry, label each one with the owner's name using a black marker. (Or have the youngster do it.) Have each child cut out his handprints. Then use all of the handprints to make a rainbow arch across the bulletin board. Title the bulletin board "We Can Make A Rainbow."

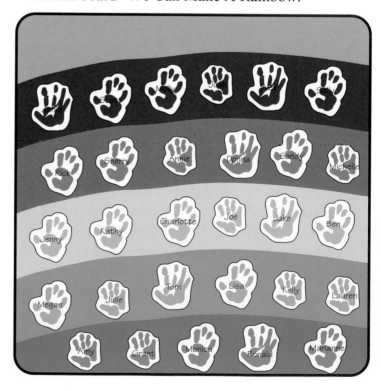

SNACK

Shape Snacks

Try these yummy snacks as a fun follow-up activity. Your little ones will just love these snacks in various shapes.

Circle—Ritz crackers, banana slices, apple rings, pepperoni slices, pickle chips, or any round cookie

Triangle—nacho chips, pizza slices, or cheese cut into triangles

Square—Wheat Thins, saltine crackers, or finger Jell-O squares

Rectangle—Club crackers, graham crackers, meat sliced into rectangles, or granola bars

CULMINATING ACTIVITY

Prepare a scavenger hunt in your classroom. Collect eight different objects with unique colors and shapes (red heart-shaped cookie cutter, yellow star-shaped puzzle piece, blue rectangular building block, etc.). Place the objects around the classroom. Then make a worksheet that has a picture of each of the eight shapes with the appropriate color word printed beside the picture. Give each child a copy of the worksheet and instruct him to search for the objects on his own. When he finds an object, have him return to his seat and color the corresponding shape with the correct color. (Children should be encouraged not to show others the location of any of the objects.) Place a time limit on the activity and when time is up, have the children reveal where each object was hidden. Children will enjoy the challenge of this activity, and you will enjoy watching them at work.

51

Colors And Shapes

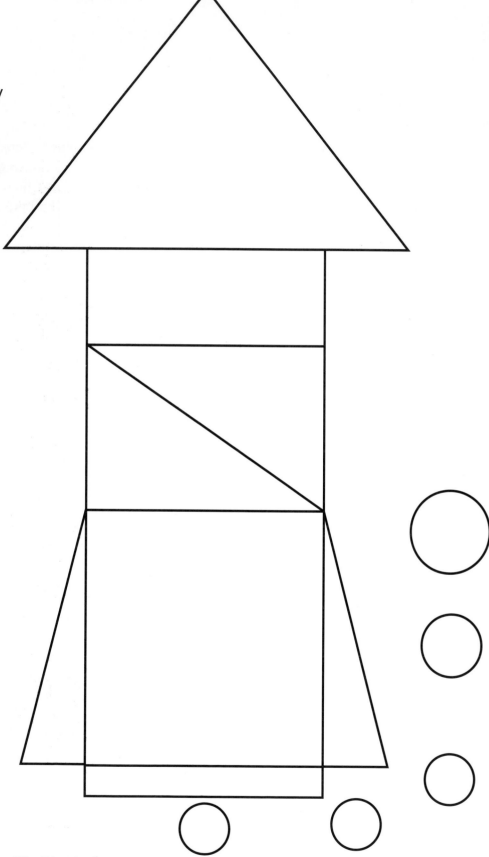

— red

— yellow

— blue

— green

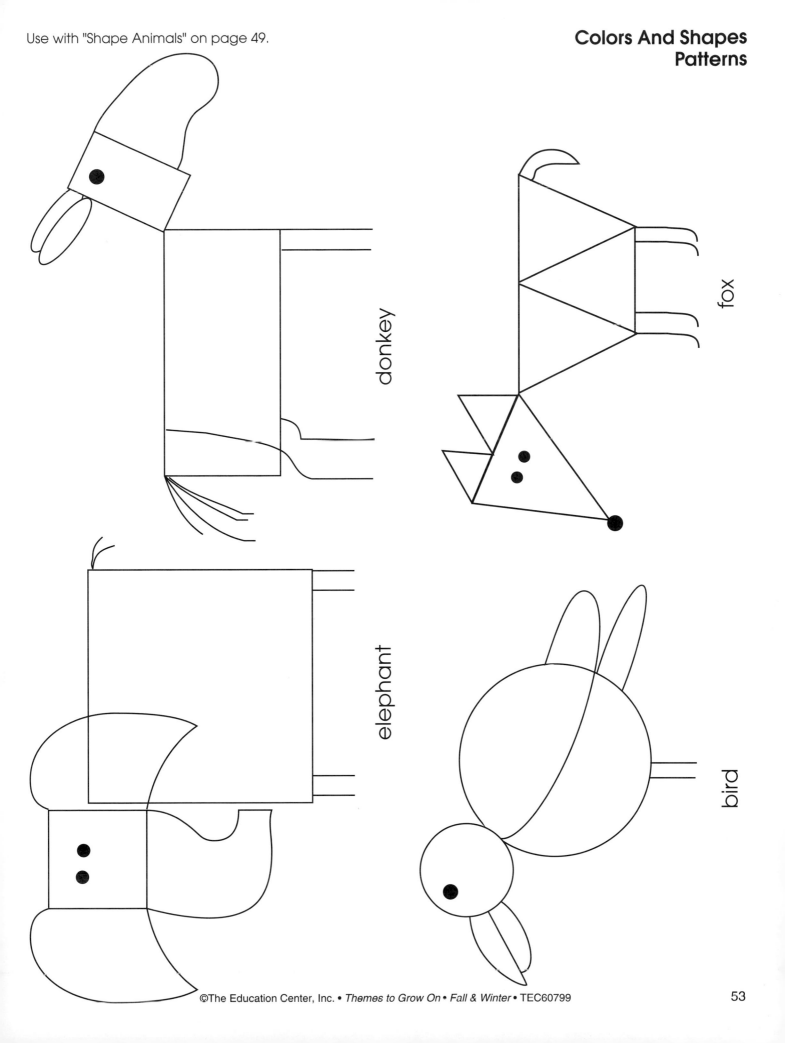

donkey

fox

elephant

bird

Farm Animals

Put on your best overalls, join the hayride, and travel the dusty roads to a farm. A barnyard filled with animal sights and sounds awaits you at the end of the journey.

MATH

Counting Critters

Make several copies of the farm animal cards on page 62. Mount the cards on tagboard. Then make a set of numeral cards using the numerals one through nine. Laminate both sets of cards for durability. Place the cards in a learning center. Have each child in the center choose a numeral card and place the appropriate number of farm animal pictures beside it. To vary the activity, use plastic farm animals instead of the farm animal cards.

To Market, To Market!

Set up an egg market in your classroom with plastic eggs, several pennies, and a large basket. First put a blank sticker or a small piece of tape on each egg. Then use a permanent marker to write a price on each egg, and place the eggs in the basket. Place the basket in a learning center. Give each child in the center ten paper pennies to use at the egg market. Tell him that he must spend all ten of his pennies when purchasing eggs. Then let him make his choices. When everyone in the center has had a chance to shop for eggs, have the children compare their purchases to see who got the most for his money, who got the least, etc.

54

Farm Animals

Weight

Reproduce the farm animal cards on page 62. Color the animals and attach the cards to a sheet of tagboard. Laminate and cut apart the individual cards. Glue a piece of felt to the back of each card. Place two cards side by side on a flannelboard. Encourage children to look at the pictures of the animals. Have them tell which animal would weigh the most and which would weigh the least. Repeat this with different combinations of cards.

Animal Patterning

Use the duplicated farm animal cards made for the "Counting Critters" activity on page 54 to play a patterning game. First have children in a small group sit in a semicircle. Then place all of the cards faceup in front of the children. Begin a simple pattern by selecting a few of the cards and placing them in a line. Have children in the group take turns adding cards to the line to make a pattern. Repeat this procedure, creating several new patterns. Then let children use the cards to make original patterns.

Ordinal Positions

Make ribbons similar to those awarded to winners at a county fair (the color of each place winner is listed below). Then make a poster listing the ordinal positions first through ninth. Beside the word for each ordinal position, glue a piece of ribbon of the appropriate color. Attach the poster to a wall or chalkboard. Review the ordinal positions and ribbon colors with the children. Then have nine children stand in a line and pretend that they are winners at a county fair. Ask the children remaining at their seats to tell which child would receive the red ribbon, yellow ribbon, etc. As each child is named, give her the appropriate ribbon. Repeat the activity using a different group of children.

first—blue
second—red
third—white
fourth—pink
fifth—yellow

sixth—dark green
seventh—light green
eighth— brown
ninth—gray

☐ first—blue
☐ second—red
☐ third—white
☐ fourth—pink
☐ fifth—yellow
☐ sixth—dark green
☐ seventh—light green
☐ eighth—brown
☐ ninth—gray

55

LANGUAGE ARTS

Listening

Set up a listening center in the classroom using a taped reading of *The Little Red Hen*. Give each of the children in the center a copy of the book *The Little Red Hen*. Ask him to follow along in his book as he listens to the tape. Then have children act out the story (simple masks representing each of the characters in the story may be used). Conclude by providing the group with a small loaf of bread to be sliced and served to each child.

Clipping Initial Consonant Sounds

Use a marker to divide a cardboard circle into eight sections. Glue a picture of a different farm animal in each section. Write the beginning sound of each animal on an individual clothespin. Have a child in a learning center clip each clothespin to the part of the wheel picturing the animal with the name that begins with that sound. *(Note: The clothespins and the back of the circle may be color coded to make the activity self-checking.)*

Dramatic Play

Read *Big Red Barn* by Margaret Wise Brown. Then have child volunteers act out the story while the remaining members of the class reread the book.

Choral Reading

Print the text from, *"Quack!" Said The Billy Goat* by Charles Causley on a large sheet of chart paper. Read the poem to the class. Then ask the class to read it with you. Divide the class into several small groups. Assign each of the small groups a different part of the poem to read and have the class read the poem as a choral reading. Videotape children as they read the poem. Then, at a later time, show the children the video.

Wishy-Washy Language Experience

Read *Mrs. Wishy-Washy* by Joy Cowley. Then ask children to think of other farm animals that might have been included in the story. Write the name of each animal on a sheet of chart paper. Next have children dictate for you to write a story about Mrs. Wishy-Washy that includes most of the animals on the list. Ask children to follow the format of *Mrs. Wishy-Washy.* Rewrite each sentence on a separate sheet of construction paper. Have each child illustrate a sentence and bind the pages together to create a class book. Record the original story *Mrs. Wishy-Washy* on one side of a cassette tape. Then have the children record their version on the other side of the tape. Place the tape, copies of *Mrs. Wishy-Washy,* and the class book in a listening center.

Sequencing

Read *Hattie And The Fox* by Mem Fox. Discuss the sequence of events in the story. Then give each child a copy of the pictures on page 63. Have her cut out the pictures. Assist the children as they correctly sequence the pictures on a strip of construction paper. Have them glue the pictures in place.

A Walk With Rosie

Read *Rosie's Walk* by Pat Hutchins to a small group of children. Point out each of the position words used in the story (*across, around, over, past, through,* and *under*). Then have children follow you on a course set up in the classroom that is similar to the one taken by Rosie. Listed below are some suggestions for the course layout.

across the yard—Walk across the floor.
around the pond—Walk around a piece of blue paper placed on the floor.
over the haystack—Walk over a small stool or wooden box.
past the mill—Walk past a door.
through the fence—Walk between two chairs.
under the beehives—Crawl under a table.

SCIENCE

Farm Animals

Introduce children to farm animals and their young by reading *Farm Animals* by Karen Jacobsen or *Baby Farm Animals* by Merrill Windsor.

Animal Products

Make poster board cutouts of a cow, sheep, goose, and chicken. Have children discuss various products derived from each of the four animals. Then let each child look through an old magazine. Ask him to cut out pictures of some of the products mentioned in the discussion. Glue each of the pictures to the animal cutout.

Making Butter

Give each child in a small group a clean baby food jar. Pour one-fourth cup of whipping cream into the jar. Secure the lid tightly. Have her vigorously shake the jar until the cream solidifies into butter. Serve the homemade butter on crackers and enjoy them. Hint: The butter will form faster if the jars are refrigerated to make them cold before using.

SOCIAL STUDIES

Field Trip

An excellent way to acquaint children with farm animals is to take them on a field trip to a local county fair or an animal farm equipped to handle visitors.

Farming Fun

Draw a map of a farm on a large sheet of paper (include a barn, silo, pond, pigpen, chicken coop, pasture surrounded by a fence, garden, road, and farmhouse). Color the map with markers and laminate it for durability. Place the map and several small plastic farm animals in a learning center. Let the children in the center play with the farm set, placing the animals in various locations on the map.

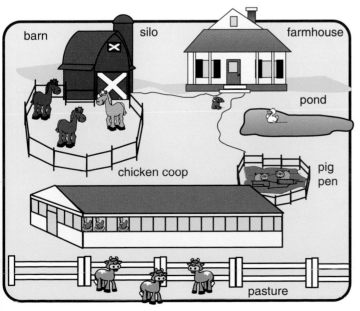

barn silo farmhouse
pond
chicken coop pig pen
pasture

Farm Animal Trivia

List the names of several male, female, and baby farm animals on a sheet of paper (such as sow—female pig, gander—male goose, piglet—baby pig, etc.). Call out the animal names one at a time. Have children identify each name by describing the animal.

Farm Workers

Contact the Agricultural Extension Service or local 4-H representative to find people willing to talk to your class about the various jobs on an animal farm.

Dairy Farm

Read *The Milk Makers* by Gail Gibbons. Then take children on a field trip to a dairy farm. Use a camera to take several snapshots of the different parts of the farm. Glue each of the snapshots on an individual sheet of paper. Write a caption below each snapshot. Bind the papers together to create a class book. To vary this activity, have each child draw a picture of his favorite part of the dairy farm. Then ask him to think of a sentence to describe his drawing. Have him write or dictate for you to write his sentence at the bottom of the picture. Bind the papers together to make a book.

A cow licked salt from my hand.

ART

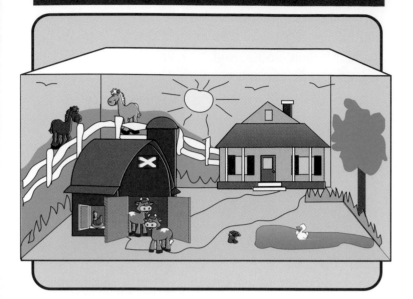

Shoebox Diorama

For homework, ask each child to use her imagination and create a farm scene inside a shoebox. Tell her that the background can be colored with markers or painted. Toy farm animals and fences can be used along with straw, grass, or similar materials. A barn, silo, chicken coop, and farmhouse may be drawn on separate pieces of paper and attached to the sides of the shoebox. Ask each child to share her shoebox diorama with the class on the day that it is due. Then place the dioramas on display in the classroom, space permitting.

Bulletin Board

Cover a large bulletin board with a beautiful farm scene. First staple a piece of light blue paper to the top of the bulletin board to make the sky. Then cut out mountains from dark green, brown, and tan paper. Staple the mountains onto the blue background. Attach a piece of green paper to the bottom of the bulletin board to create the pastureland. Make a pond from blue paper and a road from brown paper, and attach both to the green paper. Then, on separate sheets of paper, draw a barn, silo, fence, sun, farmhouse, and small garden. Paint them with tempera paints, cut them out, and staple them to the background paper. Make patterns for horses, cows, chickens, pigs, sheep, and ducks. Place the patterns in a learning center. Ask each child in the center to select a pattern. Have him trace around the pattern, paint the animal shape, and cut it out. Then let him attach the following material to his animal to make it look 3-D. Staple each child's animal to the bulletin board to complete the farm scene.

chicken and duck—small feathers
horse—yarn for mane and tail
pig—pink pipe cleaner for curly tail, pink button for snout
cow—thumbprints made from black tempera for spots, black yarn for tail
sheep—cotton balls

SNACK

Making Bread

After reading *The Little Red Hen,* have children participate in making bread. Use a boxed bread mix or the following recipe for soft pretzels:

Soft Pretzels

1 package yeast
1 1/2 cups warm water
1 teaspoon salt
1 tablespoon sugar
4 cups flour
salt

Dissolve the yeast in the warm water. Add the salt, sugar, and flour. Knead the dough until smooth. Twist the dough to form letters, numbers, or shapes. Brush them with water and sprinkle them with salt. Bake at 425° for 12 to 15 minutes.

CULMINATING ACTIVITY

Barn Dance!

Read *Barn Dance!* by Bill Martin, Jr. and John Archanbault. Then have your children prepare for an old-fashioned classroom hoedown. Ask each child to come to school the following day dressed as a farmer. He may wear overalls, a flannel shirt, work shoes, a straw hat, a bandana, etc. As children arrive in the classroom on the day of the hoedown, have each of them construct a unique paper-plate mask of a farm animal to use with the day's activities. Then have the children sing their favorite farm songs, imitate farm animal movements, and recite farm poems. End the day by serving a snack of juice and animal crackers.

Farm Animals
Animal cards
Use with "Counting Critters" on page 54, "Weight" and "Animal Patterning" on page 55.

 ©The Education Center, Inc. • *Themes to Grow On* • *Fall & Winter* • TEC60799

Apples

An apple a day turns work into play! Apple play in math, language arts, science, social studies, and art will keep your class smiling through the day. Bushels of fun-filled learning experiences await your youngsters as you bite into this "apple-tizing" unit on apples.

MATH

Counting With Apples

Duplicate the apple pattern on page 72 several times on red construction paper. Write a numeral and/or corresponding number word on each apple. Laminate for durability. Place the apples and small containers of raisins in a learning center. Have children place the correct number of raisins on each apple. Allow children to eat the raisins when the activity has been completed.

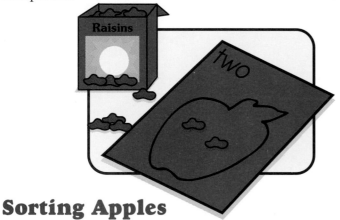

Sorting Apples

Ask each child to bring an apple to school. Put the apples in a bushel basket or box. Place the container of apples in a learning center. Have children sort the apples by color and size.

Estimation Apple Station

Give each child in a small group a piece of paper. Show him a red, a green, and a yellow apple. Have him use crayons to draw each of the three apples on his paper. Then encourage him to estimate the number of seeds in each one. Have him write the estimated number beside the appropriate drawing. Cut open the apples and count the seeds. Compare the number of seeds in each apple with children's estimations.

Apple Weighing

Place a set of scales, a cup of crayons, and an assortment of apples and another cup in a learning center. Ask children to weigh each apple using the scales and several crayons. After each apple is weighed, have children count the number of crayons used. Let them determine which apple weighed the most, the least, etc.

More And Less

Use the apple pattern on page 72 to make several apples from construction paper. Punch a different number of holes in each apple using a hole puncher. Then divide an overhead projector screen in half by drawing a line from top to bottom. Write the word *Left* on the top left of the screen and the word *Right* on the top right. Place an apple on each side of the screen. Have children count the number of "worm holes" in each apple. Then ask children to tell which apple has more worm holes and which apple has less. Repeat the activity using a different pair of apples.

Apple Seed Counting

Clean ten baby food jars and the lids. Place the lids on the jars. Use a screwdriver to punch a hole in each lid large enough for an apple seed to fit through. Put a blank sticker on the front of each jar. Then use a marker to write a numeral on each sticker. Place the jars and a container of apple seeds in a learning center. Have children in the center put the correct number of seeds into the jars.

Apple Graphing

Make a large graph with drawings of a red apple, a green apple, and a yellow apple on the left-hand side. Attach the graph to a wall or chalkboard. Then show children examples of the three apples pictured on the graph. Ask children to sample a slice of each type of apple and describe how it tasted. Then let each child decide which apple she liked best. Give her a drawing of an apple. Let her color the drawing the color of her favorite apple. Have her cut out the apple and attach it to the graph beside the apple that matches her own. Conclude by counting the apples in each row and deciding which type was the most liked by the majority of the children.

Getting Your Apples In Order

Use the apple pattern on page 72 to make several apples from green construction paper. Write a different numeral on each apple. Laminate for durability. Attach a piece of felt to the back of each apple. Place two apples on a flannelboard. Ask children to tell which numeral would come before the pair and which would come after. Then place two new apples on the board. Have children tell which numeral would go between the pairs. Repeat the activity using different combinations of numbers.

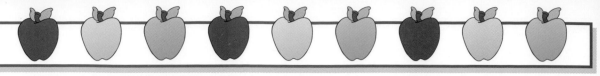

LANGUAGE ARTS

Cooking Up A Recipe Book

Have children think of different foods that are made from apples. List the foods on chart paper. Then ask each child to bring a favorite apple recipe from home. Compile the recipes into a recipe book (include apple recipes used in the classroom). Make a copy for each child.

Describing Apples

Make an apple booklet for each child in the class. Enlarge the apple pattern on page 72. Use the pattern to make a front and back cover from red construction paper. Staple three pieces of paper inside the cover. At the bottom of each page, write the sentence, "Apples are _____." Next give each child an apple to observe and taste. Have her describe the various features of the apple (size, shape, color, weight, texture, etc.). List each of the descriptive words on chart paper. Then give her a copy of the apple booklet. Ask her to choose three of the descriptive words from the list. Complete the sentences by writing one of the words in each of the blanks. Let her use crayons to draw an illustration in the space above each sentence.

Ending Sounds

Duplicate the apple pattern on page 72 several times on red construction paper. Cut each apple in half horizontally. Draw or paste a picture of an object on the top half of each apple. Then write the ending sound for each object on the bottom half of the apple. Laminate for durability. Put the apple puzzles in a box. Place the box in a learning center. Have children in the center complete the puzzles by matching the objects to the ending sounds.

Storytelling

Below is a folktale about the star in the center of an apple. Tell the story to children using a flannelboard and a figure of each of the characters in the story.

The Little Red House With No Doors

Once upon a time there was a little boy who was tired of playing with his toys. He said, "Mother, I am bored. What can I do?"

His mother said, "Go outside and find a little red house with no doors or windows and a star inside."

So the little boy went outside to search for the house. There he met a little girl. "Do you know where I can find a little red house with no doors or windows and a star inside?" he asked the girl.

"No, I don't," said the girl, "but my father may know."

So the little boy asked the girl's father, "Sir, do you know where I can find a little red house with no doors or windows and a star inside?"

The girl's father laughed, "No, Boy, I have never seen anything like that. Go ask Grandmother. She has lived a very long time and is very wise. Maybe she will know."

So the little boy asked Grandmother, "Please, can you tell me where I can find a little red house with no doors or windows and a star inside?"

"No," said Grandmother, "but I would like to find that house myself. Go ask the wind; he knows everything."

The wind blew by the little boy and the little boy asked, "Oh, Wind, do you know where I can find a little house with no doors or windows and a star inside?"

The wind said, "Yes, Boy. I will show you the way." The little boy followed the wind up a grassy hill. At the top of the hill was an apple tree. The wind blew the tree and an apple fell off. "Look on the ground, Boy, and you will find your house," said the wind.

The boy looked on the ground and picked up the apple. "It's a little red house with no doors or windows, but where is the star?" asked the little boy.

The wind replied, "Take it home and ask your mother to cut it in half." The little boy hurried home to his mother.

"Mother, I have found the little red house with no doors or windows. Please cut it in half so that I might see the star." The little boy's mother took a knife and very carefully cut the apple in half. Inside was a star holding tiny brown seeds.

—Author Unknown

At the conclusion of the story, cut an apple in half horizontally and show the children the star.

67

Vocabulary Words

Draw three views of an apple (uncut, cut horizontally, and cut vertically) on a large poster board. Ask children to identify the different parts of the apples. Write the name of each part on the poster. Draw a line from the name to the corresponding part of the apple.

We Like Apples

Introduce this activity once the graphing activity on page 65 has been completed. Working in small groups, let each child complete the sentence, "I like _____ apples," filling in the blank with the word *red, green,* or *yellow.* Write each sentence on chart paper. The next day, using the same small groups, let each child find his sentence on the chart. Ask him to read the sentence aloud. Then give him a strip of paper with his sentence printed on it. Ask him to cut apart the sentence, separating it between each word. Have him glue the words in the correct order at the bottom of a sheet of paper. Let him draw a picture of the apple he liked best on the paper above his sentence. Bind the papers together to create a class book.

SCIENCE

Graphing Apple Snacks

On each of the first four days of the apple unit, provide a different apple snack for children to enjoy. Listed below are suggested snacks.

Monday—raw apple slices
Tuesday—apple juice
Wednesday—apple butter or apple jelly on bread
Thursday—applesauce

Prepare a graph with a picture of each of the four snacks on the left-hand side. Give each child an apple cutout with her name printed in the center. Ask her to choose her favorite snack. Then have her attach the apple cutout to the graph beside the picture of the apple snack she liked best. Count the number of children who liked each of the four snacks and compare the amounts.

Our Favorite Apple Snacks			
apple slices	Tina		
apple juice	John	Kiesha	Tonya
apple jelly on bread	Zach	April	
applesauce	Todd	David	Beth

Sequencing

After discussing the growth of an apple tree, give each child a copy of the pictures on page 73. Have her color the pictures and cut them apart. Then ask her to glue the pictures in the correct sequence on a strip of construction paper.

Preserving Apples

Cut an apple in half. Rub one half with lemon juice. Do nothing to the other half. After a few hours, have children observe and compare the appearance of the two halves.

69

SOCIAL STUDIES

Community Workers

Contact the Agricultural Extension Service in your county to obtain the name of a person who works with apples and is willing to share his expertise with children. You also may wish to inquire about someone with an apple press who can make apple juice, someone who makes apple pies or apple turnovers, or an apple farmer.

Johnny Appleseed

Introduce children to the story of Johnny Appleseed by reading *Johnny Appleseed Goes A Planting* by Patsy Jensen.

ART

Apple Printing

Cut two apples in half vertically and two in half horizontally. Place the apple halves in a learning center. Give each child in the center a piece of white construction paper and containers of red, yellow, and green tempera paint. Have him dip an apple half in the paint and make prints on the construction paper.

Sponge Painting

Give each child in a learning center a piece of white construction paper and a brown strip of paper. Have her tear along the edges of the strip to create a paper tree trunk. Ask her to glue the tree trunk in the center of the white construction paper. Next give each child a container of green tempera paint and a small sponge. Have her dip the sponge into the tempera paint and sponge paint leaves above the tree trunk and grass below it. Then give her a container of red tempera paint. Have her dip a finger into the tempera paint and paint apples on the tree and a few below it.

Papier-Mâché

Have each child in a learning center crumple a piece of newspaper into a ball the size of an apple. Place several paper-towel strips and a container of papier-mâché mix in the center. Let each child dip paper-towel strips into the papier-mâché mix and use them to cover the ball of newspaper. Allow the papier-mâché apples to dry completely. Then let each child paint her apple with red, yellow, or green tempera paint. Insert a small stick into the top of the apple to make the stem. Then use a hot glue gun to secure the stick to the apple. Place completed apples in a large basket and use it as an attractive display in the classroom.

SNACK

Apple Snack

This is a nutritious apple snack that children will enjoy.

  6 apples
  1/2 cup crunchy peanut butter (or soy nut butter)
  1/4 cup wheat germ
  1/4 cup nonfat dry milk
  2 tablespoons honey

Wash and core the apples. Combine the remaining ingredients. Stuff the mixture into the center of the apples. Slice the apples horizontally. Serves 12–18.

CULMINATING ACTIVITY

Conclude the unit on apples in the spirit of Johnny Appleseed. Have the children make apple bags for faculty and staff members. Give each child a brown paper lunch bag. Ask her to make an apple print on the front of the bag (see "Apple Printing" on page 70). When the paint has dried, let her place an apple and a note inside the bag. Then have her deliver the apple bag to a teacher or staff person.

Apples Pattern

Use with "Counting With Apples" on page 64, "More And Less" and "Getting Your Apples In Order" on page 65, and "Describing Apples" and "Ending Sounds" on page 66.

©The Education Center, Inc. • *Themes to Grow On* • *Fall & Winter* • TEC60799

Stop, look, and listen! Use the following ideas to enable your students to take a big step toward learning the importance of safety in their everyday lives.

MATH

Parts Of A Whole

Purchase a set of cardboard traffic signs from an educational supply store. Laminate the signs for durability. Cut each sign apart to make a puzzle. Put all puzzle pieces in a box and place in a learning center. Have children in the center use the puzzle pieces to re-create the traffic signs.

Matching

Make several copies of the safety signs on page 82. Color each sign and laminate for durability. Then cut apart individual safety signs. Put signs in a box and place the box in a learning center. Ask children in the center to match the signs that have the same shape or color.

Phone Home

Make a copy of the telephone pattern on page 83 and laminate for durability. Use a grease pencil to write the telephone number of each child in the rectangular shape at the bottom of a telephone pattern. Then write the numerals zero through nine on individual index cards and place in a box. Give each child the telephone with her phone number printed at the bottom and seven paper squares or buttons. Assign a student volunteer the task of being the telephone operator. Ask the operator to pick one numeral card at a time from the box and read it aloud. Let each child with that numeral cover it with a paper square or button. When a child has covered all the numerals in her telephone number, have her call out, "Hello." Shuffle the numeral cards, choose another operator, and play again.

Counting Order

Make a traffic light for each child in a learning center from a strip of black construction paper and glue on a red, a yellow, and a green circle. Then cut out several circles from white construction paper. Write a numeral on each white circle. Laminate traffic lights and paper circles for durability. Place sets of three sequentially numbered circles in individual bags. Have each child in a learning center place the set of numerals in counting order on a traffic light. One hint: to make the activity self-checking, color code the back of each circle according to the order of the lights on a traffic light.

LANGUAGE ARTS

Brainstorming

On the first day of the unit, have children think of safety rules that apply to fire, water, traffic, home, and school. Write each set of rules on a separate piece of chart paper. Post charts in the classroom until the conclusion of the unit. Add new rules to the appropriate chart each day.

Vocabulary Words

Mount a large picture of a fire truck, fire fighter, police officer, or police car on a piece of chart paper. Attach the chart to a wall or chalkboard. Have children take turns identifying or describing objects in the picture. Use a marker to write the name of each object on the chart paper. Then ask a child to draw a line from the word to the corresponding object in the picture. Conclude the activity by writing a sentence about the picture at the bottom of the chart.

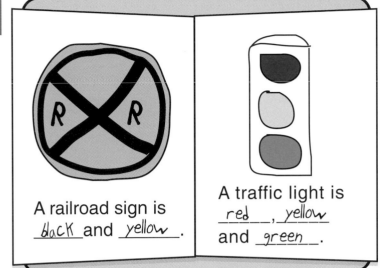

A railroad sign is
black and _yellow_ .

A traffic light is
red , _yellow_
and _green_ .

Signs, Signs!

Let each child make a traffic sign book. Give him a folded piece of construction paper to make the book cover. Have him trace or draw traffic signs on the cover. Each day, give him a sheet of paper with the following sentence (below) printed at the bottom. Ask him to write the correct color words in the blanks. (Give younger children a plastic bag with all the color words needed to complete the book. Have them select the appropriate words each day and glue them in the blanks.) Have each child draw a picture of the traffic sign above each sentence.

    Monday—A stop sign is _____ and _____. *(red, white)*
    Tuesday—A yield sign is _____ and _____. *(red, white)*
    Wednesday—A hospital sign is _____ and _____. *(blue, white)*
    Thursday—A railroad sign is _____ and _____. *(black, yellow)*
    Friday—A traffic light is _____, _____, and _____. *(red, yellow, green)*

Safety Rules Are Cool

Each day, allow children to draw a picture of a safety rule being followed. Write the rule that each child's drawing illustrates on her picture. (Have older children copy the rule from one of the safety charts posted in the classroom.) Bind the pictures together to create individual safety books.

fire hat

fire hose

yellow

boots

Fire fighters put out fires.

75

SCIENCE

Fire And Air

Secure a candle in the bottom of each of two clean mayonnaise jars. Punch three or four holes in the lid of one of the jars. Light the candles in both jars. Then place the lids on the jars. The candle inside the jar with the holes punched in the lid will continue to burn. The candle inside the jar with no holes in its lid will go out. Tell children that fire cannot burn without air. Then ask them to think about how a fire extinguisher might work and discuss it.

Hearing

Tape-record several warning and safety sounds (school fire drill alarm, smoke detector alarm, car horn, police whistle, etc.). Play the tape for the class. Help children identify the source of each sound. Then discuss the importance of knowing what to do when each sound is heard.

Lotto Sign Game

Duplicate the sign patterns on page 82. Choose nine of the signs. Color and mount these in a three-by-three configuration to form a lotto board. Duplicate four construction-paper copies and laminate. Cut apart two of the copies for playing cards and reserve the other two intact for gameboards. To play the lotto game, have pairs of children stack the playing cards between them. Each child, in turn, draws a card and matches it to his board. The first to fill his board wins. If he chooses a duplicate card he puts it at the bottom of the stack.

To make a Concentration sign game, duplicate four construction-paper copies as before, laminate, and cut them apart. To play, place all cards facedown and have students take turns turning over two cards, attempting to find the matching signs.

SOCIAL STUDIES

Safety Rules

Each day of the unit, focus on one area of safety, using the topics below and on pages 78 and 79. Included under each topic are basic rules to discuss and one or more activities designed to reinforce the discussion.

Fire Safety

1. Never play with matches.
2. If your clothing catches on fire, remember to stop, drop, and roll.
3. To avoid smoke, stay low and go.
4. Keep away from hot appliances.
5. Practice home fire drills.

Take the class on a field trip to a fire station. Arrange to have a fire fighter give them a tour of the facility and discuss the importance of fire safety.

Water Safety

1. Never swim alone.
2. In a boat, stay seated and wear a life jacket.
3. Get out of the water during thunderstorms.
4. Walk around a pool.
5. Learn to swim.

Tell the class that they will play Water Safety Charades. First model play acting each water safety rule. Divide the class into pairs. Assign each pair a different water safety rule. Ask one child to pretend to be someone who is following the rule and the other child to pretend to be someone who is breaking the rule. Have the remaining members of the class guess which rule is being demonstrated.

Always stay seated in a boat and wear a life jacket.

See page 77 for how to use these topics.

Traffic Safety

1. Obey all traffic signs and lights.
2. Always fasten your seat belt.
3. Before crossing a road, look left, right, and then left again.
4. Listen and follow directions from the bus driver.
5. Keep both hands on the handlebars when riding a bike.

Arrange to have a school bus brought to your school. Have the driver describe the important safety features of the bus. Then ask him to discuss the proper behavior for children while riding a bus. Have the bus driver take your class on a short trip to practice the rules they have learned.

Invite a police officer to bring his police car to school. Ask the officer to show the children his car and review general traffic rules for cars and bikes.

School Safety

1. Walk in the hallways.
2. Keep your hands and feet to yourself.
3. Keep litter in its place.
4. Stay alert and play safe on the playground.
5. Do not play with fire alarms or fire extinguishers.

Have a member of the school safety patrol or the principal come and talk to your class about school safety rules.

Take your class on a safety hunt throughout the school. Talk about safety in each of the following areas: the bus loading zone, hallways, stairways, playground, cafeteria, and classroom.

See page 77 for how to use these topics.

Home Safety

1. Know your home phone number and street address.
2. Do not take pills or medicine unless your parents give it to you.
3. Stay away from household cleaners.
4. Never open the door for strangers.
5. Attach emergency phone numbers near each phone in the house.

Describe several situations that could happen in the home and have children tell what will happen next. Listed below are a few suggestions.

- You left several toys on the stairs. Your mother is carrying a large load of laundry and has started walking down the stairs. What will happen next?

- Your mother accidentally left the door open to the cabinet where the household cleaners are stored. You see your baby brother sitting beside the cabinet opening a bottle of cleaner. What will happen next?

- You are at home by yourself. You hear the doorbell ring. You look out a window to see who is at the door, but you do not recognize the person. What will happen next?

- While walking home from your friend's house, you take a wrong turn and get lost. A police officer stops you and asks if she can help. What will happen next?

ART

Mobile

Reproduce the safety signs patterns on page 82 for each child in a learning center. Have him color and cut out the signs. Then ask him to tape the end of a piece of yarn to the back of each sign. Tie the safety signs to a clothes hanger to create a mobile.

Thank-You Cards

Give each child in a learning center a sheet of paper and a straw. Drop a small amount of diluted tempera paint in the center of each sheet of paper. Ask each child to use his straw to quickly blow the paint across the paper. Repeat the procedure using different colors of tempera paint. Allow the paint to dry. Then have each child fold his paper in half to make a note card. Ask him to write a thank-you note inside the card to one of the resource people who visited the class during the safety unit. Mail all note cards to the respective visitors.

Safety Vehicles

Place an assortment of small boxes, containers of tempera paint, and several paintbrushes in a learning center. Let each child in the center choose a box. Ask him to paint the box to resemble a safety vehicle (police car, fire truck, ambulance, etc.). Then have him glue the appropriate number of black cardboard circles to his vehicle for the wheels once the paint is dry.

School Bus

Draw a large school bus on yellow paper. Use black paint to color in the wheels, make stripes on the side, write a number on the front, etc. Cut around the outline of the bus once the paint is dry. Then cut a row of windows in the side. Attach the bus to a bulletin board or wall in the hallway. Then have each child paint or draw a picture of her face and cut it out. Place a few of the faces in each bus window. Then cover the windows with a piece of plastic wrap.

SNACK

Traffic Light Cookies

Make traffic light cookies in a small group setting.

    slice-and-bake sugar cookie dough, softened
    canned white frosting
    red, green, and yellow food
        coloring

Roll out cookie dough that has been softened slightly. Cut out a 2" x 5" rectangle from the dough for each child in the group. Place dough rectangles on a cookie sheet and bake. Then divide the frosting into three containers. Add red, green, and yellow food coloring respectively to the containers of frosting. Have each child use a Popsicle stick to spread small circles of the frosting on her cooled cookie.

CULMINATING ACTIVITY

Safety Questionnaire

Prepare a safety questionnaire for each child to take home and complete with the help of a parent. When the questionnaires have been returned, allow the children to compare their responses.

Questionnaire

Fire
1. Is there a smoke detector in your home? ❑ yes ❑ no
2. Has your family practiced a fire drill at home? ❑ yes ❑ no

Water
3. Can you swim? ❑ yes ❑ no
4. Do you get out of the water during thunderstorms? ❑ yes ❑ no

Traffic
5. Do you wear a seat belt when riding in a car? ❑ yes ❑ no
6. Do you wear a helmet when riding your bike? ❑ yes ❑ no

Home
7. Do you know your home phone number? ❑ yes ❑ no
8. Do you know the emergency phone number? ❑ yes ❑ no

School
9. Do you walk in the hall? ❑ yes ❑ no
10. Do you play safely on the playground? ❑ yes ❑ no

Safety Patterns

Use with "Matching" on page 74, "Lotto Sign Game" on page 76, and "Mobile" on page 80.

 ©The Education Center, Inc. • *Themes to Grow On* • *Fall & Winter* • TEC60799

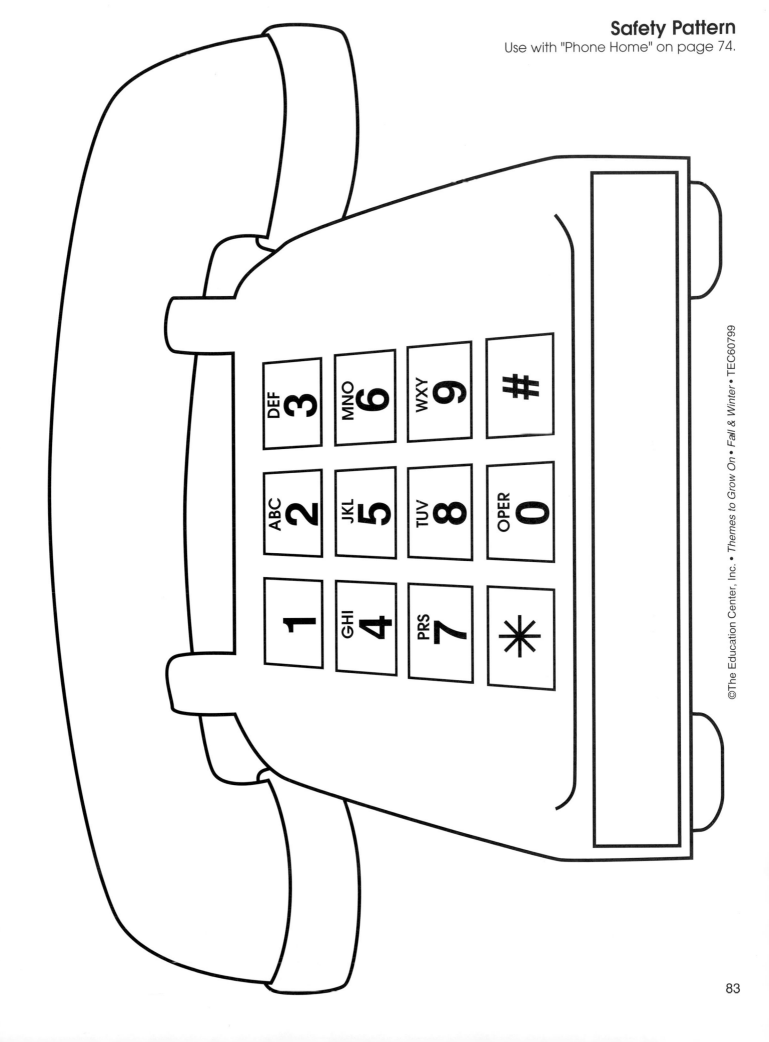

©The Education Center, Inc. • *Themes to Grow On • Fall & Winter* • TEC60799

Seasons

It's winter! It's spring! It's summer! It's fall! Take a peek at each season and have a ball! Your youngsters will learn about various climates and times of the year while journeying through the seasons.

MATH

Number Sequence

Give each child an outline of a thermometer and an old magazine or newspaper. Have him look for the numerals 1 through 20 in the reading material. Ask him to cut out the numerals and paste them in the correct sequence on the thermometer.

Categories

Place several pieces of clothing in a large box. Have children in a learning center separate the clothing into four smaller boxes by season. Listed below are clothing suggestions. At the conclusion of the activity, allow the children time to dress up in the clothing.

Summer
sandals
flip-flops
swimsuit
shorts

Winter
knit cap
scarf
mittens
coat

Spring
sweater
baseball cap
short-sleeved shirt
sneakers

Fall
jacket
long-sleeved shirt
sweat shirt
long pants

Mr. Thermometer

Tape an outdoor thermometer outside on a window so it is visible indoors. Each day, read the temperature outside and post the number on a wall or bulletin board. During the week, compare the posted temperatures. Discuss which day had the highest temperature, the lowest, etc.

Calendar Counting

Use a class calendar to reinforce counting. Each day have children sit in a semicircle around the calendar. Then ask children questions similar to those listed below.

How many days are in this month?
How many Sundays (or other days) are in this month?
How many days are there until the next holiday?
On which day does the month begin (end)?
How many days are there until our next field trip?
How many birthdays are in this month?
How many days until the new month begins?

Ordinal Position Words

Print the ordinal position words *first* through *twelfth* on individual strips of tagboard. Code strips on the backs with the numerals 1 through 12, respectively. Then print the name of each of the months on an individual tagboard strip and code the backs for self-checking. Laminate both sets of word cards for durability. Place cards in a learning center. Have children in the center match and sequence the two sets of cards.

Graphing

Make several copies of the seasons cards at the top of on page 92. Cut apart the individual cards. Then, on the last day of the unit, let each child choose the season that is her favorite. Give her a copy of the card that represents the season she likes best. Have her attach her card in the appropriate place on a graph.

LANGUAGE ARTS

Seasonal Reading And Writing

Begin the unit by reading *Caps, Hats, Socks, And Mittens: A Book About The Four Seasons* by Louise Borden. Then lead the class in a discussion about events that are associated with each of the four seasons. Make a list of the events on four separate sheets of chart paper and label each list with the name of the corresponding season. Add ideas to each list during the week as children learn more about the four seasons.

Language Experience

Focus on a different season each of the first four days of the unit. On each day, allow each child time to complete a page for an individual book about seasons. For example, on the first day, give each child a piece of paper with the sentence, "In spring I _____," printed at the bottom. Have her think of an ending for the sentence, using the ideas listed on the appropriate seasons chart (see "Seasonal Reading And Writing"). Ask her to illustrate the sentence at the top of the paper. Then go around the room while the children are drawing and have each child dictate the ending to you. Print her words in the provided space. Repeat the activity on the following three days, substituting a different season in each of the sentences. On the fifth day, give each child a piece of paper with the sentence, "My favorite season is _____," printed at the bottom. Have her complete the sentence and illustrate it. Bind each child's papers inside a cover to create an individual seasons book.

My favorite season is ___fall___.

Soupy Poetry

Read aloud *Chicken Soup With Rice* by Maurice Sendak. Then divide the class into four groups. Have each of the groups rewrite the first sentence from three of Sendak's poems. For example, have one group complete the following sentences: "In January it's so nice _____," "In February it will be _____," "In March the wind _____." Write each sentence on chart paper as it is dictated by children. Then copy each sentence on an individual sheet of paper. Let children illustrate the sentences. Bind the papers together to create a class book.

Chicken Soup With Rice

Cinquains

Divide the class into four groups. Then, using the following outline, help each group write a cinquain about a different season. Print each cinquain on a separate piece of chart paper or large seasonal cutout. Let each group share its cinquain with the rest of the class. Copy the cinquains on individual sheets of paper. Bind the papers together to create a class book.

Line 1 contains 1 word.
Line 2 contains 2 words.
Line 3 contains 3 words.
Line 4 contains 4 words.
Line 5 is the same as Line 1.

SCIENCE

Matching

Give each child a copy of the matching worksheet on page 93. Have him match the pictures of the children to the corresponding seasonal pictures at the top of the page.

The Four Seasons Table

At the beginning of the unit, send home a schedule of the week listing the day each season will be discussed. Ask children to bring in objects or pictures associated with each season on the assigned day. Then divide a large table into four sections. Attach a piece of poster board to the wall above each section. Print the name of a different season on each piece of poster board. Glue seasonal pictures to the appropriate poster and place seasonal objects below the poster on the corresponding section of the table. Leave the display up until the end of the unit.

Season In A Box

Place several related objects in four shoeboxes (see suggestions listed below). Give each child in a small group one of the boxes. Ask her to look inside the box and describe each of the objects. Let the remaining group members guess the names of the objects described. Then ask children to tell which season is in the box. Continue in the same way until all four boxes have been shared.

Spring
package of seeds
artificial flower
plastic Easter egg

Summer
sunglasses
sand shovel
flip-flops

Fall
acorn
apple
fall leaf

Winter
mitten
package of hot chocolate
Christmas tree ornament

Temperature

Obtain four shallow, metal pans. Fill one with hot water, one with warm water, one with cool water, and one with cold water. Arrange the pans in order from hot to cold and label them accordingly. Then show children a thermometer. Point out the red line that marks the temperature. Place the thermometer in the pan of hot water. Have children watch the change in the red line. Ask children the following questions: Did the red line go up or down when placed in the first pan of water? Do you think the air in our room is hotter or colder than the water in the first pan? How do you know?

Shake the thermometer and place in the pan of warm water. Then ask children the following questions: Did the red line change? How? Is the water in the second pan hotter or colder than the water in the first pan?

Continue this activity with each pan of water. Then conclude by asking children the following questions: What happens to the red line as the temperature goes from hot to cold? From cold to hot? Which pan had the highest temperature? Which pan had the lowest temperature? Discuss the various temperatures and their changes from season to season.

Note: A large demonstration thermometer with an adjustable red band can be purchased from a school supply store. The demonstration thermometer can be attached to a wall or chalkboard and used in conjunction with the temperature activity. The use of the demonstration thermometer allows each child to see the temperature measured by the glass thermometer.

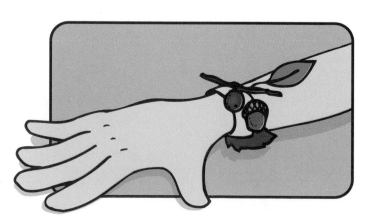

Fall Bracelet

Tape a piece of masking tape (sticky side out) loosely around each child's wrist. Then take the class on a nature walk. While on the walk, have each child find small objects (leaves, twigs, acorns, etc.). Ask him to attach the objects to his fall bracelet.

SOCIAL STUDIES

Weatherperson

Invite a local television or radio weatherperson to share information with your class about the special services he provides for the community and the weather associated with each season.

Seasonal Pictures

Collect several pictures of people participating in seasonal activities such as swimming, building a snowman, raking leaves, and planting a garden (an old calendar is a good source). Attach each picture to a piece of tagboard and laminate for durability. Cut each one into four or five strips. Place the strips in a container. Have the children in a small group sort the strips and place them in the correct order to re-create each picture. Afterwards ask the youngsters to describe the activities and name the seasons pictured.

Seasonal Actvities

At the beginning of each season, send home a list of activities each child can do with a parent or other family member (see suggestions below).

Winter
drink hot chocolate
make a snow angel
watch a football
  game
give a gift
build a snowman

Spring
make a bird feeder
fly a kite
hide Easter eggs
plant a flower
make a grass whistle

Summer
go swimming
watch fireworks
eat ice cream
blow bubbles
play catch

Fall
jump into a pile of leaves
carve a pumpkin
go on a nature hunt
make a leaf rubbing
write a thank-you note

Four Seasons

On the last day of the unit, divide the class into four groups. Secretly assign each group one of the four seasons. Give each group a piece of poster board and a few old magazines. Ask group members to cut out pictures that represent their assigned season and glue them to the poster board. At the conclusion of the activity, have a representative from each group show the poster to the class. Let class members guess which season is represented by the poster.

89

ART

Puzzle

Give each child in a learning center a copy of the grid pattern on page 92. Ask him to draw and color one large seasonal picture over the entire grid. Next have him cut the picture apart on the grid lines. Let him place the picture pieces in a plastic bag. Then have children exchange and work each of the picture puzzles.

Seasonal Painting

Place paper, tempera paint, and paintbrushes in a learning center. Then have the children in the center paint a seasonal picture while listening to a portion of Vivaldi's *The Four Seasons* or selections from Tchaikovsky's *Nutcracker Suite*.

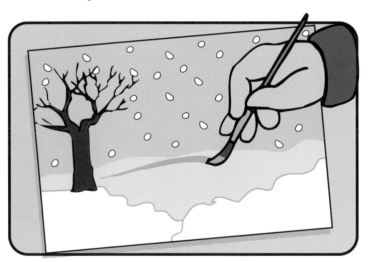

Seasonal Banner

Give each child in a small group a rectangular piece of solid-colored fabric. Provide fabric paints. Ask her to paint a seasonal picture on the fabric. Allow the paint to dry. Then place the fabric piece right side down on a table. Place a wooden dowel at the top of the fabric and one at the bottom. Fold the fabric over each dowel. Use a hot glue gun to secure the fabric around each dowel. Then use two thumbtacks to attach a piece of yarn to the ends of the top dowel.

Seasonal Hats

Have each child in a learning center create a hat for the Four Seasons Pageant (see "Culminating Activity" on page 91). Place several poster-board strips in the center. Let each child choose a strip and paint it with finger paint. Then have her decorate the strip with materials representative of one of the four seasons, such as the following:

spring—plastic or silk flowers
summer—bright-colored crepe-paper streamers
fall—twigs, acorns, small pinecones
winter—cotton balls, Styrofoam packing pieces

Finally fit the strip around the child's head and staple the ends together.

SNACK

Seasons Kabob

Let each child create a Seasons Kabob by sliding a fruit associated with each of the four seasons onto a wooden skewer.

    winter—orange section
    spring—strawberry
    summer—raspberry
    fall—apple slice

CULMINATING ACTIVITY

Four Seasons Pageant

Practice for a Four Seasons Pageant to be presented to parents or another class at the conclusion of the unit. Divide the class into four groups. Assign each group one of the four seasons. Have each group learn one or two seasonal poems and a seasonal song. Let each child create an appropriate hat (see "Seasonal Hats" on page 90) and/or costume for the pageant. Then have the children perform.

Seasons Patterns

Use with "Graphing" on page 85.

Use with "Puzzle" on page 90.

©The Education Center, Inc. • *Themes to Grow On* • *Fall & Winter* • TEC60799

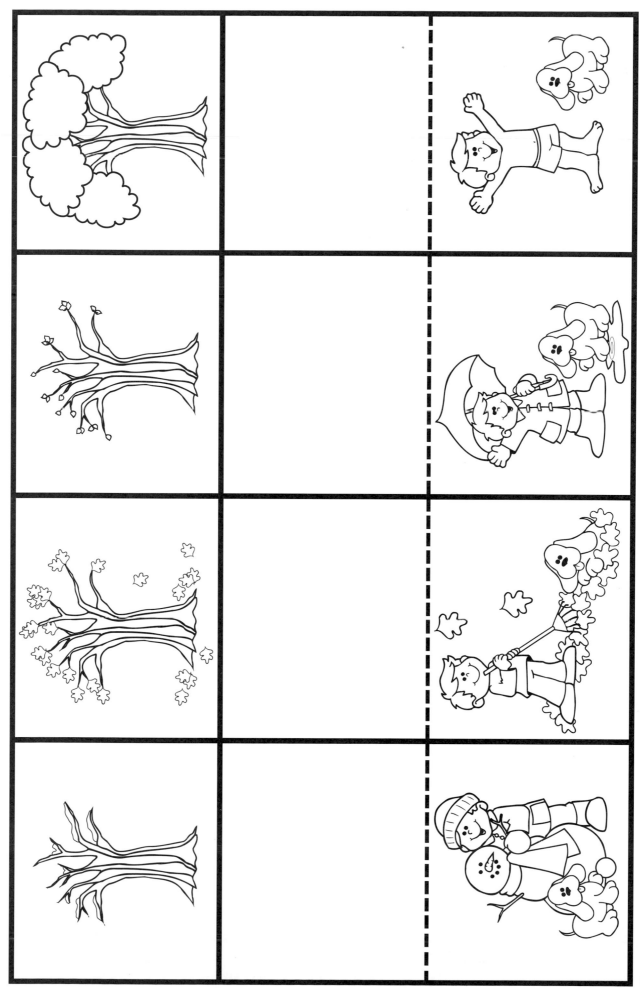

Name _____

Seasons Matching

Use with "Matching" on page 87.

©The Education Center, Inc. • *Themes to Grow On* • *Fall & Winter* • TEC60799

Birds

Children's natural interest in and familiarity with birds will be excellent motivations for this unit. Share with children the following basic skills concepts that relate to our fine feathered friends.

MATH

Counting Birdies

Cut several cards from tagboard. Use an ink pad and a rubber bird stamp to print from one to five birds on each card. Arrange the birds differently on each card. Place the completed cards in a basket. Have the children in a learning center match the cards that have the same number of birds.

Birds Of A Feather

Make several copies of the bird and feather patterns on page 102. Cut out the bird and feather patterns. Print a different numeral on each bird. Write a number sequence or addition/subtraction problem on each of the feathers. Laminate the birds and feathers. Place them in a learning center. Have the children in the center match the feathers to the corresponding birds.

Weighing Eggs

Fill four plastic eggs with objects of different weights such as thumbtacks, cotton balls, beans, buttons, or clay. Tape around the middle of each egg to secure the contents. Then have children in a learning center sequence the eggs from lightest to heaviest. Let children use a beam scale balance to judge the weights of the eggs, or have them decide by holding the eggs in their hands. For easy checking, number the eggs.

Ordinal Positions

Label the sides of ten paper cups or butter tubs with the ordinal position words *first* through *tenth*. Turn the containers over sequentially in a straight line and hide a jelly bean under one. Have the children in a learning center take turns guessing which container is covering the jelly bean. Lift each container as it is guessed. If the jelly bean is not under the container that is guessed, turn it right side up. If the jelly bean is under the container, begin the game again. Vary the activity by not turning over the container if a guess is incorrect.

Nests And Eggs

Label ten butter tubs with the numerals one through ten. Put Easter grass in each tub to make the tub resemble a bird's nest. Place the containers and a bag of jelly beans (eggs) in a learning center. Have the children in the center put the correct number of jelly beans in each butter tub. Vary the activity by labeling a number word instead of a numeral on each butter tub.

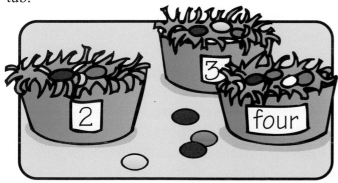

Shape Birds

Have each child in a learning center create a bird using basic geometric shapes. Place construction-paper scraps, glue, scissors, pencils, and patterns for the following shapes in a center: circle, oval, triangle, square, rectangle. Let each child trace and cut out the shapes he needs. Then have him glue them on a sheet of construction paper to create a unique shape bird.

Graphing

Make a class graph using pictures of five or six birds common to your area. Each day that the children go outside to play, have them look for those birds. When the children come inside, ask them to indicate which birds they saw. Color in a square beside each bird spotted by one or more of the children. At the end of the week, count and compare the numbers of birds observed by the children.

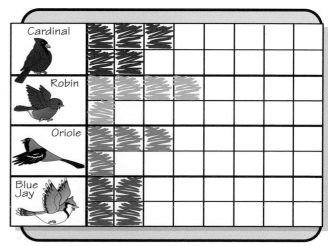

95

LANGUAGE ARTS

All About Birds

Read and discuss factual books about birds on the first three days of the unit. On the fourth day, have the children discuss the facts they have learned about birds. List each fact on chart paper or a large bird cutout. Choose three or four of the facts and print them on individual sheets of paper. Make a copy of each page for each child in the class. Ask him to illustrate the pages. Then bind the pages together to create individual bird books.

Fine Feathered Friends

Make several copies of the bird and feather patterns on page 102. Color and cut out the birds. Write a different letter on each feather. Laminate the birds and feathers. Place sets of five sequential feathers in individual plastic bags. Give a bag of feathers and a bird to each child in a learning center. Ask her to place the feathers in alphabetical order on the bird. Have her exchange feathers with another child in the group and begin again.

ALL ABOUT BIRDS by Chris

Birds lay eggs.

A duck is a game bird.

Choral Reading

Obtain a big book of *Good-Night, Owl!* by Pat Hutchins. Number or color-code the lines in the book as follows:

Use the number 1 or the color yellow for the names of the animals.

Use the number 2 or the color red for the animal sounds.

Use the number 3 or the color blue for the phrase, "…and Owl tried to sleep."

Divide the class into three groups. Assign each group a number or color. Have each group read the appropriate line on each page. Point above the words as children read. Have the students practice reading the book several times. Record their choral reading on an audio- or videocassette.

Dramatization

Good-Night, Owl! by Pat Hutchins can be easily dramatized by your youngsters. Assign each child an animal from the book to draw on one half sheet of construction paper. Punch a hole in each corner at the top of the paper. Insert yarn in the holes and tie the yarn around a child's neck. Each child then acts out the part of the character he is wearing as you reread the story. For added fun and a nifty character display, insert a tree branch in a bucket of sand. Hang the character pictures from the branch when finished with the story.

Language Experience

If birds could talk, what would they say? Ask your children to respond to each of the following questions. Write each of their answers on chart paper. Then let the children vote on the answer they liked best for each question. Make a class big book using the favorite response to each of the four questions. Finally ask the children to illustrate the big book in a learning center.

What would a bird say to a bug?
What would a bird say to a squirrel?
What would a bird say to a scarecrow?
What would a bird say to you?

Story Stretching

As a follow-up activity to reading *Good-Night, Owl!* by Pat Hutchins, have the children write a class book with a similar story line. Let the children choose a person or animal to substitute for the owl. A farm animal, jungle animal, or class pet would make an excellent choice. Have the children think of the noises that would keep the main character from sleeping. The children may suggest sounds made by animals, people, vehicles, or machinery. Have each child choose one of the noisemakers and dictate a sentence about how it keeps the main character from sleeping. The format of the sentences should be similar to those in *Good-Night, Owl!* Write each sentence on chart paper as it is dictated. Copy each sentence on an individual sheet of paper and have each child illustrate his sentence. Bind the pages together to create a class book.

SCIENCE

Garlands

Have the children string different types of garlands for birds to eat. Hang the garlands on a tree near the classroom. Check the garlands each day to see which one the birds eat first, second, last, etc. Foods recommended for the garlands include: dried fruit, peanuts in the shell, cranberries, stale popcorn, CheeriOs, and Fruit Loops.

Nifty Nests

Take the children on a nature walk. Have them look for things that a bird might use to make a nest such as twigs, pieces of string, dried grass, straw, and leaves. Place all of the items found in a potato or onion sack. Poke the materials through any openings or holes in the bag so part of them are visible. Tie the sack to a tree. At the end of the week, check the bag to see which of the items are missing.

Science Center

Encourage your youngsters to bring in items associated with birds such as abandoned bird nests, feathers, eggshells, and factual books about birds and eggs. Place the items in a science center and provide a magnifying glass. Have small groups of children visit the center during the week to examine the items on display.

Sequencing

Many educational supply catalogs carry science sequencing cards that picture the life cycle of birds, birds building nests, birds hatching from eggs, and so on. These cards may be used by the teacher to illustrate various aspects of bird life, or they may be placed in a learning center for independent practice in sequencing.

Bird Feeders

Have each child make a bird feeder to take home or hang outside the classroom. Included below are directions for three types of bird feeders. Choose the one that best suits your needs.

Bread Feeder—Give each child in a learning center a piece of bread and a cookie cutter. Have him use the cookie cutter to cut out a shape from the slice of bread. Have him use a straw to punch a hole at the top of the shape. Have him brush one side of the bread shape with egg white and sprinkle it with birdseed. Allow the bread to dry completely. String yarn through the hole to make a hanger.

Pinecone Feeder—Give each child in a small group a pinecone and a pipe cleaner. Have her wrap one of the pipe cleaner around the top of the new cone and bend the free end to form a hook. In a bowl, mix together peanut butter or soy nut butter and some birdseed or suet and birdseed. Have each child use a tongue depressor to press some of the mixture onto the pinecone scales.

Suet Feeder—Cut several squares from onion or potato sacks. Give each child in a learning center one of the squares. Mix suet (available in most supermarkets) and birdseed in a bowl. Have each child placc a large spoonful of the suet mixture in the center of the net square. Have him tie the four corners of the square together with a piece of yarn.

SOCIAL STUDIES

Bird Caretakers

Invite a veterinarian, pet shop owner, or parent to bring a pet bird to your classroom. Ask the visitor to discuss the bird's care and eating and sleeping habits.

Homes Are Special

Show the class pictures of various nests built by birds. Let the children point out the similarities and differences in the nests. Then discuss how the different nests meet special needs of the birds that build them. Discuss how people, like birds, have different homes to meet their needs.

Helpful Birds

Have the children brainstorm several ways birds help people (they eat harmful insects, they make beautiful music, they help scatter seeds, etc.). List each child's response on a sheet of chart paper. Then have the children imagine a world without birds. Help the children write a descriptive sentence beginning "A world without birds would be_____."

ART

Branch Weaving

Take a group of children on a nature walk. Have each child find a small branch with three or four smaller branches shooting out from it. Assemble the group around a table on which you have placed several pieces of bright-colored yarn. Have each child choose a piece of yarn and tie it to the bottom of one of the branches. Have him wrap the yarn around the other branches, moving up the branch as he works. Several pieces of yarn may be needed to reach the top of the branch. Have him tie the end of the yarn to the branch once the branch is covered. Have him weave things such as twigs, feathers, strips of paper, string, and grasses through the yarn strands.

Wallpaper Birds

Have each child in a learning center choose a large scrap of wallpaper or Con-Tact paper. Supply a bird-body pattern for the students to trace. Have each student use scissors to cut out the body of a bird from the paper. Have her use different scraps of wallpaper, pieces of construction paper, or stickers to create the bird's eye(s), beak, tail feathers, and wings. Have her attach the bird's body to a large piece of construction paper and attach the body parts to the bird.

Birdseed Ornaments

Give each child in a learning center a small piece of waxed paper and a bottle of glue. Have her squeeze the glue on the waxed paper to create a design and lay a paper clip so it sticks one half out of the top of the ornament. Have her sprinkle birdseed over the glue. Allow the glue design to dry overnight. Have each child carefully peel away the waxed paper. Have her tie a piece of ribbon or string to the paper clip at the top of the birdseed ornament and hang it in a window.

Splatter Paint Birds

Obtain several shoeboxes. Cut a piece of construction paper to fit in the bottom of each box. Make several bird patterns from poster board. Give each child in a learning center one of the shoeboxes and a bird pattern. Have him place the pattern on the paper in the bottom of the box. Secure a piece of wire screen over the top of each shoebox. Give each child an old toothbrush and a container of paint. Have him dip the toothbrush in the paint and gently rub it over the wire screen. The paint will splatter on the paper surrounding the bird pattern. Remove the wire screen and allow the paint to dry. Remove the bird pattern from the paper and the paper from the bottom of the box. Have each child mount his splatter paint bird on a large piece of construction paper to create a frame for the picture.

Punch Birds

Duplicate the bird and wing patterns on page 103 on construction paper. Give each child in a learning center a copy of the patterns and a pushpin. Have the child place a piece of Styrofoam or a thick piece of cardboard under his paper. Under close supervision, have him carefully use the pin to punch holes in the dots on the bird's body and wing. Have him cut out the body and the wing and then glue the wing to the bird's body. Use a hole puncher to punch a hole in the top of the bird. Tie a string through the hole and hang the birds in a window so the sunlight will shine through the holes.

SNACK

Bird Nests

1 package (12-oz.) semisweet chocolate chips
1/2 cup chunky peanut butter (or soy nut butter)
1 can (6-oz.) chow mein noodles
Jelly beans

Put the chocolate chips and peanut butter into a microwave-safe bowl. Microwave them for 1 1/2 minutes. Remove and stir the mixture. Microwave for an additional minute or until the chocolate chips have melted. Add the chow mein noodles. Stir until the noodles are evenly coated. Place heaping tablespoons of the mixture on a sheet of waxed paper and shape into nests. Let the "nests" cool slightly. Then add a few jelly beans to each one. Let them cool completely before removing them from the waxed paper.

CULMINATING ACTIVITY

Bulletin Board

Create an attractive bulletin board with milk-carton birdhouses and paintings of various birds. Collect several small milk cartons. Wash out the cartons and let them dry. Then use an X-acto knife to cut away one side of each carton. Staple the top of the carton together and spray paint it. Next have each child in a small group draw a picture of a bird on a sheet of construction paper and cut it out. Attach the birdhouses to a bulletin board. Then staple the cut-out birds inside, on, and around the birdhouses.

Bird Patterns

Use with "Birds Of A Feather" on page 94 and "Fine Feathered Friends" on page 96.

©The Education Center, Inc. • *Themes to Grow On* • *Fall & Winter* • TEC60799

Pumpkins

Tiptoe through the pumpkin patch and harvest a roomful of centers and activities that extend learning and promote cooperation.

MATH

Pondering Pumpkins

Cut open a pumpkin and let the children look inside at the many seeds. Ask each child to estimate the number of seeds he sees. Record each response on chart paper or on a large pumpkin cutout. Count the pumpkin seeds to see who had the closest estimate. Save the seeds for additional unit activities.

Prize Pumpkins

Demonstrate how to measure the circumference of pumpkins of various sizes by using a ball of string. Hold one end of the string on the pumpkin. Wrap the string around the pumpkin. Cut the string at the point where the two ends meet. Hold up the string so the children can see its length. Then show the children another pumpkin. Have each child estimate the circumference of the pumpkin by cutting a piece of string that he thinks is long enough to go around the widest part of the pumpkin. Have each child use his string to measure the actual circumference and then tell if his estimation was longer or shorter than the actual circumference.

Weighing Pumpkins

Let each child hold a pumpkin and estimate its weight. Record each child's estimate on chart paper. Place each pumpkin on a bathroom scale to find out its exact weight. Compare the exact weight with each estimate. Discuss how many estimates were less than the actual weight of the pumpkin and how many were more.

Mr. Jack-O'-Lantern

Draw one-half of a jack-o'-lantern face on a sheet of paper. Make a copy for each child. Have children complete the picture by drawing the missing parts of the face to match the other side.

Pumpkin Problem Solving

Make up several word problems related to pumpkins that are similar to those listed. Write them on large pumpkin cutouts. Read each word problem aloud and have a student volunteer raise his hand when he knows the answer.

David's pumpkin weighs 6 pounds. Jessica's pumpkin weighs 3 pounds. Whose pumpkin weighs the most?

The pumpkin farm sold 5 pumpkins before lunch and 4 pumpkins after lunch. How many pumpkins were sold in all?

Michael's pumpkin cost $10.00. Natalie's pumpkin cost $8.00. Whose pumpkin cost the least?

Keesha has 4 pumpkins. Ann has 2 pumpkins. How many more pumpkins does Keesha have than Ann?

David's pumpkin weighs 6 pounds. Jessica's pumpkins weighs 3 pounds. Whose pumpkins weighs the most

Sequencing

Give each child a copy of the pumpkin cards on page 112. Have him color each pumpkin and cut the pictures apart on the solid lines. Have him glue the pumpkin pictures in the correct sequence on a strip of construction paper and then number the pictures sequentially from one to six.

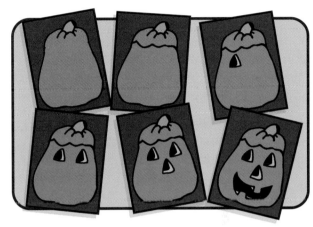

Addition

Have a group of children use a set of number cards to play a game of Make Five. Have the children sit in a circle and place the set of cards facedown in the middle of the playing area. Give each child two cards. The first child draws the top card from the stack and lays down any combination of cards that has the sum of five. At the end of the game, the child with the most combinations wins. Vary the game by giving the children three or four cards each and having them make combinations of other numbers.

LANGUAGE ARTS

A Pumpkin Story

Read aloud the book *Pumpkin Pumpkin* by Jeanne Titherington. Read it several times until the children can read along with you. Have the children create individual books with a similar format. Type or print the sentences listed below on a sheet of paper and make a copy for each child.

1—Jamie planted a pumpkin seed.
2—The pumpkin seed grew a sprout.
3—The pumpkin sprout grew a plant.
4—The pumpkin plant grew a flower.
5—The pumpkin flower grew a pumpkin.
6—The pumpkin grew and grew until he picked it.
7—Jamie carved a pumpkin face.
8—He saved six pumpkin seeds for planting in the spring.

Use a paper cutter to cut the sentences apart. On each day of the unit, have the children read the sentences printed on the strips. Have each child glue the sentence strips on separate sheets of paper and illustrate each page. Add a special touch to the book by cutting the pages and the cover in the shape of a pumpkin. Let the children illustrate pages 1 and 8 using real pumpkin seeds.

Pumpkin Relatives

Pumpkins belong to the same family as gourds, squash, watermelons, cucumbers, honeydew melons, and cantaloupes. Have the children compare the similarities and differences between a pumpkin and each of the other family members. Have the children hold and observe each of the samples. A picture may be substituted if the actual item is not available. Divide a sheet of chart paper in half. Label one side "Same" and the other side "Different." Have the children discuss similarities and differences as you list them under the appropriate heading.

Positioning Pumpkins

Give each child a sheet of paper and some crayons. Ask her to listen and watch carefully as you describe and demonstrate where to draw five different pumpkins on the sheet of paper.

Draw an orange pumpkin in the top right corner.
Draw a green pumpkin in the bottom right corner.
Draw a yellow pumpkin in the center of the paper.
Draw a red pumpkin in the bottom left corner.
Draw a blue pumpkin in the top left corner.

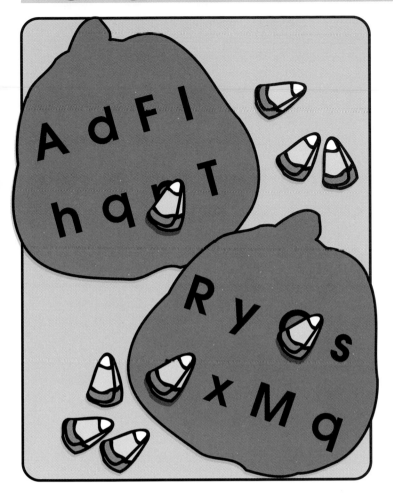

Grow, Pumpkin, Grow!

Read *The Biggest Pumpkin Ever* by Steven Kroll and "The Garden" from *Frog And Toad Together* by Arnold Lobel. Have the children brainstorm some things they could do to help a pumpkin grow to become large. Encourage them to use their imaginations, even though many of the suggestions may be unrealistic. Write the suggestions on a sheet of chart paper as they are dictated by the children. Copy each child's sentence on a sheet of paper and have him illustrate it. Older children may copy their own sentences from the chart paper. Bind the pages together to create a class book titled "How To Grow A Big Pumpkin."

Letter Recognition

To prepare for this activity, make several pumpkin cutouts from large sheets of orange construction paper. Use a black marker and write a different set of upper- and lowercase letters on each pumpkin to create a gameboard. Laminate the gameboards. Place the gameboards, a set of alphabet cards, and a container of candy corn in a learning center. Give each child a gameboard and a handful of the candy. Place the alphabet cards facedown in the center of the playing area. Turn the cards over one at a time and call out the name of the letter on each card. If a letter appears on a child's gameboard, ask her to cover it with a piece of candy corn. The child who covers all her letters first is the winner. At the end of the game, have each child name the letters on her gameboard and eat the candy corn. Shuffle the cards, have the children swap gameboards, and play again. If your time is limited, have a teaching assistant or one of the children in the center call out the letter names.

SCIENCE

Cooking

Dry the pumpkin seeds saved from "Pondering Pumpkins" on page 104 for two days on wax paper. Heat a small amount of oil in an electric frying pan. When the oil is hot, pour the pumpkin seeds in the pan. Cook the seeds until golden brown. Drain them on paper towels, sprinkle with salt, and serve.

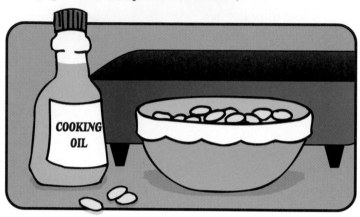

Sequencing Foldout

The children will enjoy making simple fold-out books that show the growth sequence of a pumpkin. Cut several 6" x 18" strips of paper. Fold each strip in four equal sections. Label the sections in order: "Seeds," "Vine," "Flowers," "Pumpkins." Give each child one of the fold-out books and ask him to illustrate each section.

Pumpkin Changes

What happens to a pumpkin after Halloween? Instead of throwing out the class jack-o'-lantern, keep it in the classroom in a sealed container and observe the changes it goes through as it rots. Have the children check the pumpkin regularly and take photographs or draw pictures to display on a timeline to record the changes. Some changes to look for are the following: mold, differences in colors, changes in shape.

Sprouting Indian Corn

Discover more about another harvesttime crop while learning and experimenting with Indian corn. Place an ear of Indian corn in a shallow container of water (a Styrofoam meat container works well). Check the container each day to make sure there is water in the bottom. The corn should begin to sprout in about one week.

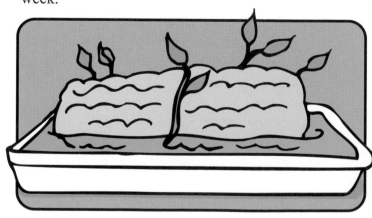

SOCIAL STUDIES

Cooperative Pumpkin Games

Use these pumpkin games to develop cooperation and sportsmanship among the children.

Scarecrow Relay—Line up your youngsters in two relay teams. Place a pile of clothes (jeans or overalls, a large shirt, a hat, and a small amount of straw) in front of each team several feet away. The first child on each team runs to the pile of clothes, puts them on, stuffs his pockets with the straw, runs back to the line, and takes off the clothes. The next child in line puts on the clothes, runs to the other end, takes the clothes off, and runs back. The relay continues until every child has had a turn.

Pumpkin Over And Under—Divide your youngsters into two lines for relay teams. In each line, have team members space themselves one arm's length apart. Give the first child in line a beach ball, a playground ball, or an orange Nerf ball. After the signal is given, the first child passes the ball over his head, the next child gets the ball, and he passes it between his legs to the next child in line. The ball is passed over and under until it reaches the last child in line. The last child takes the ball, runs to the front of the line, and continues the game. Play continues until the first child is once again at the beginning of the line.

Pumpkin Relay—Fill two pumpkin lawn bags with leaves or crumpled newspaper, and seal them. Have the first child from each of the two relay teams roll one of the bags to the opposite end of the playing area and back. Continue until all the members of the teams have had a turn. The team that finishes first wins the relay.

A Pumpkin Patch Trip

Contact a pumpkin farm in your area to arrange a field trip for your class. The children will be given a tour of the facilities and, in some cases be allowed to choose small pumpkins to take back to school.

ART

Patches Of Pumpkins Bulletin Board

Have each child participate in the creation of a classroom pumpkin patch. Have a small group of children paint several large sheets of paper with green finger paint. When the paint dries, cut out a long vine and several leaves from the paper. Attach these to a bulletin board. Have each child use a sheet of orange construction paper and a small piece of black construction paper to create a torn-paper jack-o'-lantern. Tear a black jack-o'-lantern face and glue it onto a torn orange pumpkin. Glue a small sponge square to the back of each jack-o'-lantern before attaching it to the bulletin board. This will give your pumpkin patch a 3-D effect.

Tissue-Paper Pumpkins

Give each child in a learning center two sheets of orange tissue paper and a lightweight hanger bent into a circular shape. Have him place the hanger on one sheet of the tissue paper so the hook extends past the top of the paper. Then let him glue around the inside and outside edges of the hanger. Next ask him to place the second sheet of tissue paper on top of the hanger and to press the two sheets together with the hanger in between. When the glue dries, trim the tissue paper close to the hanger. Next let the child use construction-paper scraps to create features for the pumpkin. Then hang the pumpkins on prepared vines in the classroom.

Scarecrow

A scarecrow is always a welcome addition to any pumpkin patch. Have the children make simple scarecrows using the reproducible patterns on page 113. Make several patterns out of tagboard. Use the shirt pattern to make cloth shirts from burlap. Place the tagboard patterns, burlap shirts, colored construction paper, fabric scraps, scissors, glue, crayons or markers, and tongue depressors in a learning center. Have each child use the pattern pieces to trace and cut out the parts of the scarecrow. Have him glue the parts together and attach a burlap shirt over the paper shirt. Have him cut out patches from the fabric scraps and glue them to the scarecrow's clothing. Have each child cut small, thin, construction-paper strips to resemble straw and glue them randomly on the scarecrow. Have each child use crayons or markers to draw the scarecrow's face. Finally glue a tongue depressor to the back of each scarecrow.

SNACK

Crustless Pumpkin Pie

3/4 cup sugar
1/2 cup Bisquick mix
2 tablespoons margarine
1 can (13-oz.) cvaporated milk
2 eggs
1 can pumpkin (approximately 2 cups)
2 1/2 teaspoons pumpkin pie spice
2 teaspoons vanilla

Mix all ingredients and beat until smooth. Pour the mixture into a greased pie tin. Bake at 350° for 50 to 55 minutes. Vary the recipe by pouring the mixture into small muffin tins. Bake at 350° for 25 to 30 minutes.

CULMINATING ACTIVITY

Decorated Pumpkins

For homework, have each child decorate a pumpkin to enter in a decorated pumpkin contest. Prepare a certificate for each child who enters the contest and prepare ribbons for the first-, second-, and third-place winners. Enlist the help of fellow staff members to scrve as judges for the contest. Display the decorated pumpkins in the school lobby or media center.

Pumpkin Patterns

Use with "Sequencing" on page 105.

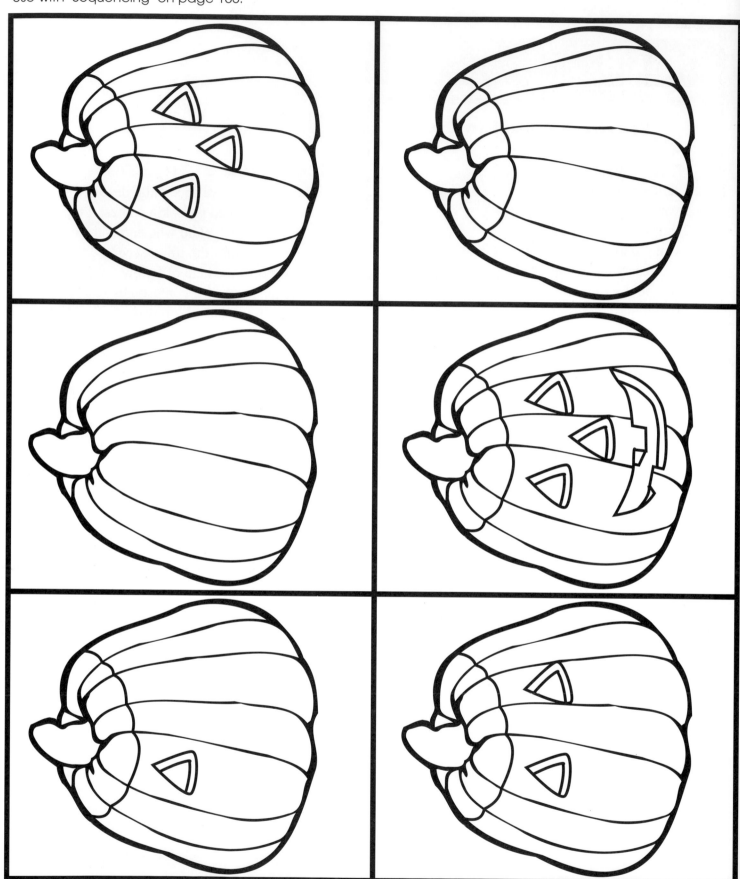

©The Education Center, Inc. • *Themes to Grow On* • *Fall & Winter* • TEC60799

©The Education Center, Inc. • *Themes to Grow On* • *Fall & Winter* • TEC60799

Dinosaurs

Present a learning playground of the prehistoric world of dinosaurs where children enhance their skills and creativity through hands-on activities.

MATH

Dinosaur Classification

Give a small group of children a variety of small plastic dinosaurs. Have the children sort and categorize the dinosaurs by color, kind, or size.

Graphing Dinosaurs

Draw a large grid on the chalkboard or a large piece of paper. Draw or attach different dinosaur pictures to the left-hand side of the grid. Have each child vote for his favorite dinosaur. Graph the responses by coloring in the squares on the grid.

Favorite Dinosaurs

Triceratops							
Apatasaurus							
Stegosaurus							
Tyrannosaurus							

Digging Up Dinosaurs

Bury several plastic dinosaurs in a sand table. Give each child in a small group an empty container. Have the children dig in the sand, find the dinosaurs, and place them in the containers. At the conclusion of the activity, have each child total the number of dinosaurs he found.

Tyrannosaurus

Give each child a copy of the tyrannosaurus reproducible puzzle on page 123. Have her color the dinosaur and cut it apart on the solid lines. Have her find the dinosaur's front, middle, and end and place them in the correct order on a piece of construction paper. Have her glue the three pieces to the construction paper.

Dinosaur Patterning

Have the children in a small group create original dinosaur patterns using scrap paper, stamp pads, and several rubber dinosaur stamps.

And Then There Were None!

Give each child in a small group ten small, plastic dinosaurs. Have her place the dinosaurs in front of her in a straight line. Have her roll a die and subtract the number that she rolled from the line of dinosaurs. Have her lay these dinosaurs down on the table or floor to show they have been subtracted. Each child in the group takes turns until someone is able to subtract all of the dinosaurs from her line. To win, the child must roll the exact number needed to have all of the dinosaurs lying down.

LANGUAGE ARTS

What's In A Name?

Write several dinosaur names on individual strips of tagboard and laminate them for durability. Give each child in a small group a grease pencil and one of the dinosaur name strips. Have a child shuffle a stack of alphabet cards and turn them facedown. Have him pick up the top card, call out the letter, and show it to the other children in the group. If a child has that letter in his dinosaur name, have him cross it out with his grease pencil. Continue until one child has all of the letters crossed out. Wipe the grease pencil marks clean with a paper towel, exchange the reshuffled alphabet cards, and begin the game again.

Dinosaur Words

Write the names of several dinosaurs on individual strips of tagboard. Cut each name apart—letter by letter—and place the letters in individual plastic bags. Give each child in a small group one of the bags and keep one for yourself. Show the children how to use the letters to spell the dinosaur name. Demonstrate ways that some of the letters in the name can be used to spell shorter words. Have the children follow your example.

If I Had A Dinosaur

Have the class listen to and discuss the song "If I Had a Dinosaur" by Raffi on his *More Singable Songs* cassette or CD. Have each child think of one thing she could do if she had a dinosaur. After each child illustrates the idea on a sheet of drawing paper, have her dictate a sentence of explanation that begins with the same words as the song, "If I had a dinosaur, just think what…." Write the sentence on the picture. Glue the picture on a larger piece of construction paper and hang it in the classroom or hallway.

Dinosaur Stories

Begin the dinosaur unit by reading *Patrick's Dinosaurs* by Carol Carrick. This book will generate an interest in dinosaurs as it combines the fictional story of Patrick with several facts about some well-known dinosaurs. Follow up the story with a discussion about dinosaurs and their physical characteristics, habitats, and eating habits.

Conclude the unit with Carol Carrick's *What Happened To Patrick's Dinosaurs?* The sequel begins with Patrick's brother explaining a few of the theories about the extinction of dinosaurs and ends with Patrick sharing his own unique idea about their disappearance. Patrick's idea will inspire the children to think of some of their own ideas which can be illustrated on drawing paper. Attach sentences of explanation dictated by the child to each drawing. The completed papers may be bound together to create a class book.

A Dinosaur Language Experience

Read *If The Dinosaurs Came Back* by Bernard Most. Discuss ways the author suggests dinosaurs could be used in the world today. Have the children think of other ways dinosaurs could be useful. Write their ideas on chart paper. Tape a large piece of white paper to a tabletop and have the children create a mural of their ideas. Copy the sentences from the chart paper onto the mural and display it in the classroom.

Dinosaurs could help us put out fires.

Dinosaurs could help us travel.

Dinosaurs could help us reach high places.

SCIENCE

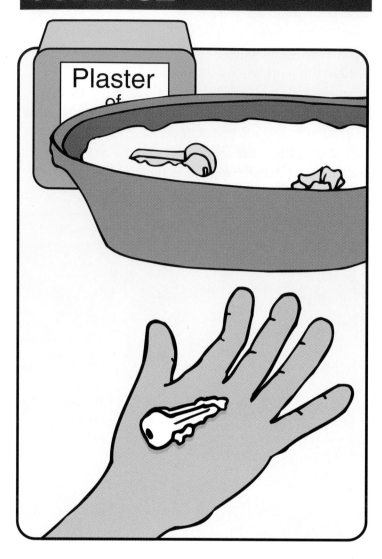

Dinoland

Involve the entire class in the creation of Dinoland. Take your class outside to a sandbox. Divide the class into three or four groups. Have the children in each group work together to make a prehistoric land complete with hills, valleys, mountains, lakes, and volcanoes. Allow the children to use nearby rocks, leaves, and sticks to add to Dinoland. Have each group use a few plastic dinosaurs to complete its model.

Fossils

Give each child in a learning center a pie tin. Have him press clay into the bottom of the tin until it reaches a one-inch thickness. If a flat surface is desired, have him pound the clay with a wooden block. Have him make impressions in the clay using a number of small objects like rocks, keys, pinecones, hair combs, etc. Remove the objects from the clay and pour plaster of Paris over the clay to a one-inch thickness. Let the plaster dry according to package directions and then remove it from the clay and pie tin. This procedure represents the process by which fossils are formed.

Volcano

Have each child in a learning center participate in making baker's clay. Give each child a portion of the clay along with a small square of cardboard. Have each child use the clay to form a volcano on the cardboard. Have her use small rocks and sticks to decorate the base of the volcano. Allow the volcanoes to air dry for three days or bake them at 300°F for one hour.

Baker's Clay

1 cup salt
1 1/2 cups warm water
food coloring
4 cups flour

Dissolve salt in warm water. To color the dough, add a few drops of food coloring. Allow the liquid mixture to cool, then add flour. Knead for ten minutes. See the directions above for how to finish these volcanoes.

SOCIAL STUDIES

Paleontologists

Fill plastic eggs (one or two more than the number of children in your class) with dinosaur stickers, rings, candy, etc. Have another class bury the eggs in a sandbox. Take your class out to the sandbox once all the eggs are buried. Have the children dig in the sand to find the dinosaur eggs.

ART

Cut-And-Paste Dinosaur

Supply each child with a copy of page 122. Divide your youngsters into groups of four. Have the children color the stegosaurus. After each child cuts apart the stegosaurus on the dotted lines, have her exchange all but one of the pieces with the other members of the group (one piece per group member). Have her glue the four pieces of the stegosaurus picture to a piece of construction paper.

Mural

Cover a large tabletop with a piece of white paper. Tape the paper to the table's sides. Draw the outline of a dinosaur mural on the paper. Use a pencil and yardstick to divide the mural into squares (at least one per child). Give each child the opportunity to choose one square and color it with crayons, chalk, markers, or paint. The mural can be displayed in the classroom or hallway.

Bulletin Board

Draw the outlines of hills, mountains, plants, rocks, and a volcano on a large piece of white paper. Have a small group of children fill in the outlines with brightly colored paint. Once the paint is dry, staple the paper to a bulletin board. On individual sheets of paper, draw different dinosaurs. Have the children fill in the outlines with paint. When they're dry, cut out each dinosaur. Staple the dinosaurs to the bulletin board, leaving a small opening between each dinosaur and the background paper. Insert crumpled newspaper in the openings and then staple them shut. The result is an attractive 3-D bulletin board the children will love!

"Sock-a-saurus"

For homework, assign each child the task of creating a make-believe dinosaur from an old sock. The sock may be an adult's or a child's. It may be any color, but it must be clean! Tell the children that they can use materials such as ribbon, buttons, ricrac, yarn, pipe cleaners, etc., to decorate their socks. Children can insert their hands into the finished socks to create puppets or they may stuff them to make toys. Have each child share his sock-a-saurus with the class on the day it is due.

SNACK

Dinosaur Dig

small paper cups
plastic spoons
Gummy dinosaurs
Fruit Loops cereal

Give each child a cup and a spoon. Have her place a Gummy dinosaur in the bottom of the cup. Then let her fill the cup with the cereal. Ask her to eat the cereal down to the dinosaur.

CULMINATING ACTIVITY

Dinosaur Size

Help the children visualize the length of a dinosaur when doing this fun activity. Take the entire class out to the playground. Use a tape measure to determine the length of a particular dinosaur. Have a number of children stand behind the extended tape measure and hold hands. Demonstrate the lengths of other dinosaurs using the same procedure. Listed below are a few dinosaurs and their approximate lengths.

Brontosaurus (Apatosaurus)	70 feet
Tyrannosaurus	50 feet
Stegosaurus	25 feet
Ankylosaurus	15 feet
Compsognathus	2 feet

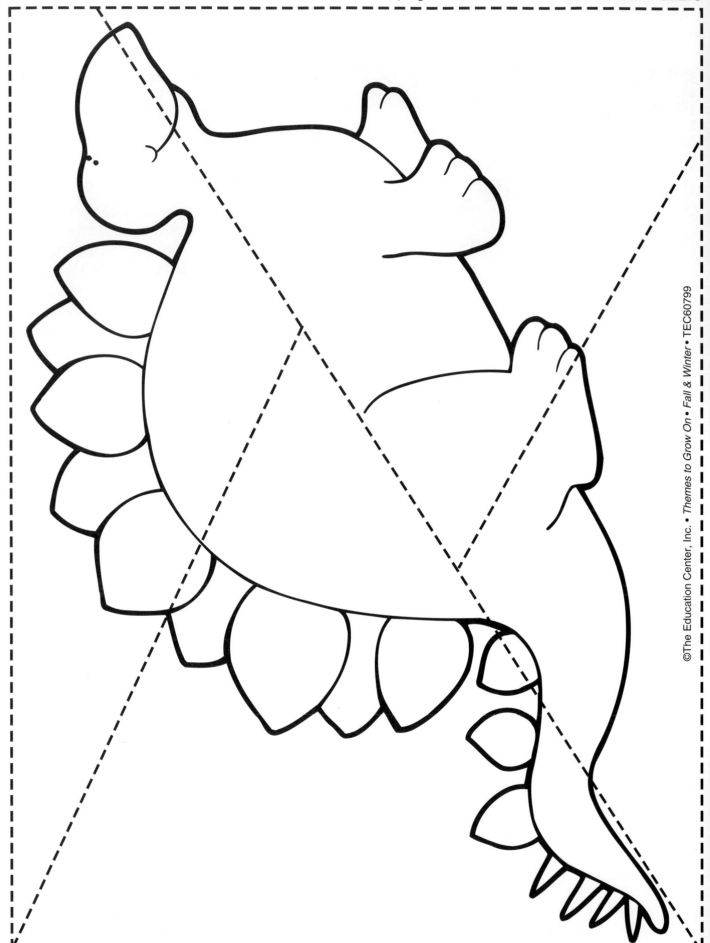

©The Education Center, Inc. • *Themes to Grow On* • *Fall & Winter* • TEC60799

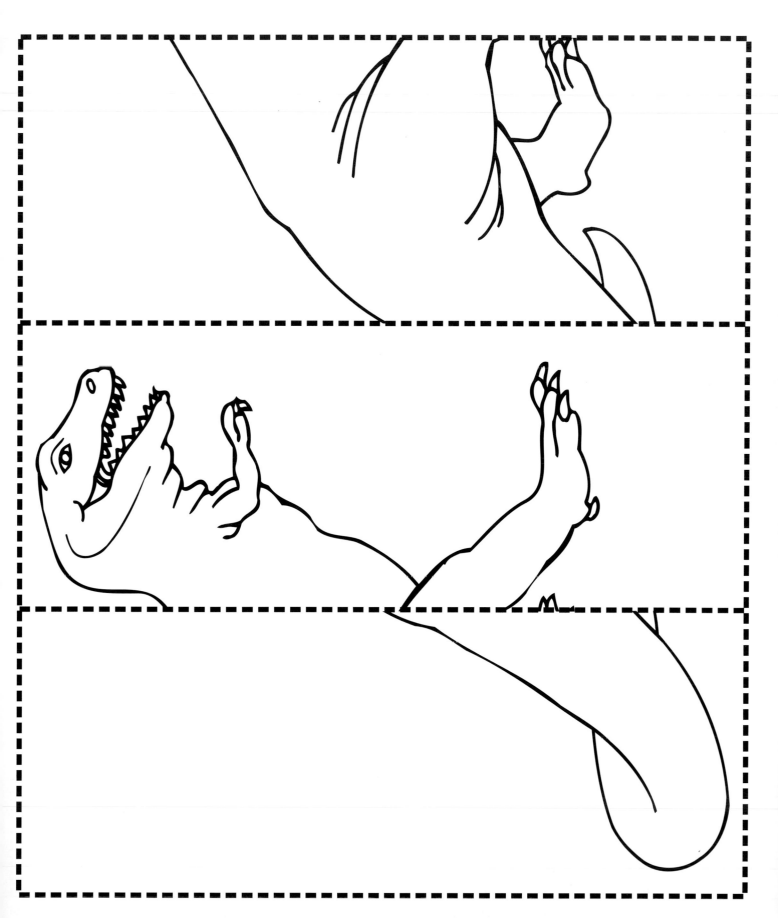

Food

Serve a smorgasbord of ideas to help your children gain a new awareness of foods and nutrition. Your youngsters will certainly have an appetite for these fun-filled activities.

MATH

Sorting Labels

Review the food groups with your youngsters. Have each youngster brainstorm a food item and then tell in which food group he would categorize the item. Then ask your youngsters to bring in food can labels such as these from tuna, corn, beans, and beef stew. Trim each label to fit a 3" x 5" index card. Glue the labels to the index cards and place the cards in a learning center. Have the children in the center sort the labels by food type.

WHERE WE SHOP

	J FOODS	FOOD USA	K Foods	BUY U MORE
6				
5	J FOODS			BUY U MORE
4	J FOODS	FOOD USA	K Foods	BUY U MORE
3	J FOODS	FOOD USA	K Foods	BUY U MORE
2	J FOODS	FOOD USA	K Foods	BUY U MORE
1	J FOODS	FOOD USA	K Foods	BUY U MORE

Grocery Store Graphing

Have the children make a graph of where their families shop for groceries. Send a note home with each child asking that he bring a logo or label from a sales circular from the store where his family normally shops. Help the children graph the results by gluing the logos on a large sheet of paper. After the logos are graphed, discuss the results.

Brown-Baggin' It!

Write a note to parents requesting that each child bring at least one—but no more than five—food items to school. Specify that the children may bring in the actual food items or labels from food boxes or cans. Attach a note to a paper sandwich bag for each child and send them home. Have each child put his food item(s) in the bag and label it. The next day, open five or six bags, one at a time. Count and describe each food item as you remove it from the bag. Put the items back in the bag and write the child's name on the outside. Later in the day, take out the same bags again. Read the names printed on the bags and ask the children to tell what was in each bag. Open the bags, one at a time, and remove the items to check for accuracy. Continue the activity throughout the unit, using a different set of bags each day.

Money

Set up a classroom grocery store in a learning center. Place plastic food, empty food boxes, and a toy cash register in the center. Price each item from one to ten cents. Have the children take turns role-playing the shoppers and store owner. Give each shopper ten paper pennies to purchase some food items. Ask the store owner to add up the cost of each shopper's items or item. Shoppers may buy additional food if money is left over from their first purchase. Once the shoppers have spent their money, have the children switch roles.

Egg Carton Counting

Using food-related manipulatives makes learning fun while giving youngsters hands-on experience. For a nifty counting activity, collect several empty egg cartons. Then use a marker to write numbers on blank stickers. Place a sticker in the bottom of each egg compartment. Put the egg cartons and a bag of dried beans in a learning center. Have each child in the center choose a carton and place the correct number of beans in each compartment. To vary the activity, write math facts on the stickers.

Coupon Bank

Send a note home with each child requesting that he bring from home food coupons that are worth 25 cents or less. Then set up a bank in a learning center with paper coins to be exchanged for the coupons. Next give each child in the center two coupons of either the same value or different values. Have the children take turns coming to the bank and picking the coin or coins that equal the amount of each coupon.

125

LANGUAGE ARTS

Classifying

Read aloud *Gregory, The Terrible Eater* by Mitchell Sharmat. Talk about the many foods that help our bodies grow and stay healthy. Discuss the foods that have little nutritional value such as junk foods. Give each child an old magazine and scissors. Have her cut out pictures of healthful foods and junk foods. Use two large sheets of poster board to display the two types of food. Vary the activity by having the children complete the cut-and-paste worksheet on page 132.

Making a Sandwich

Give your youngsters the opportunity to give you directions. Place a loaf of bread, a plate, a knife, a jar of jelly, and a damp towel on a table in front of the class. Ask the children to give you step-by-step directions for making a sandwich. Follow the children's directions exactly to demonstrate the importance of being clear and concise. For example, if one child says, "Put the jelly on the bread," then put the jar of jelly on the loaf of bread. If another child says, "No, spread the jelly on the bread," then take the knife and spread a small amount of jelly on top of the plastic bag holding the bread. Eventually, the children will give very specific directions for making a jelly sandwich.

Initial Consonant Sounds

Place a variety of foods in a paper grocery bag. Remove one item at a time. Have the children identify the item and its beginning sound. Vary the activity using pictures of different foods.

Imagining

Have the children in a learning center listen to "Aikendrum" from *Singable Songs For The Very Young* by Raffi with Ken Whiteley. Have each child use his imagination to create a picture of Aikendrum. Give him a piece of construction paper with the outline of a face drawn on the front. Allow him to choose from a variety of materials (markers, crayons, yarn, rickrack, ribbon, material scraps, etc.) to complete his picture. Have the children share and compare their portraits of Aikendrum with each other.

Cookbook Fun

Have the children make a "Favorite Foods Cookbook." Have each child dictate the recipe and cooking directions for preparing her favorite food. Copy her recipe on a sheet of construction paper and have her illustrate it. Bind the completed papers together for a class cookbook.

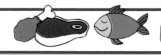  
SCIENCE

Mr. Sweet Tooth

Demonstrate how much sugar is in various foods children eat by using sugar and this story. As you share the story, spoon the amount of sugar listed after each food into a large glass jar. The children will be astonished to see the amount of sugar consumed in one day by the boy in the story.

One Saturday morning, Greg woke up and went downstairs for breakfast. He ate a bowl of Honey Smacks (4 teaspoons), a frosted Pop Tart (5 teaspoons), and a glass of chocolate milk (3 teaspoons). After breakfast, Greg went into the den to watch cartoons. About 10:30 A.M. he got hungry, so he ate a jelly doughnut (2 teaspoons) and drank a grape drink (7 teaspoons). For lunch, Greg had a bowl of Beenie Weenies (3 teaspoons), French fries (2 teaspoons) with ketchup (1 teaspoon), and an orange soda (12 teaspoons). About 3:30 in the afternoon, he decided to have a snack. He ate a candy bar (4 teaspoons) and drank a cola (10 teaspoons). For dinner, he ate a slice of pizza (4 teaspoons) and drank a glass of Kool-Aid (6 teaspoons). For dessert he ate an ice-cream sundae (19 teaspoons). That night Greg went to bed with a terrible stomachache.

Gross-Motor Skills

Place several empty junk food containers (cookie boxes, plastic soft drink bottles, Pringles cans, etc.) in a learning center. Ask the children in the center to stack the containers. Then have them take turns knocking the containers down by throwing a beanbag at the stack.

Estimating And Comparing

Have the children compare the water content in various foods. Collect a variety of fruits and vegetables (grapes, tomatoes, potatoes, celery, cucumbers, apples, oranges, squash, and carrots). Cut each fruit and vegetable into small pieces and place the pieces on paper plates. Cut several paper towels in half (the brown ones available at most schools are best). Have each child take a particular piece of food, put it on a paper towel, fold the towel over the food, and press. The water in the food will be absorbed by the paper towel. Discuss with the children the amount of water produced by the food. Continue the procedure with each of the remaining pieces of food. Compare each paper towel to see which had the most and least water absorption. Then show the children a picture of each food used in the experiment. Have them order the pictures beginning with the food that produced the least amount of water and ending with the one that produced the most.

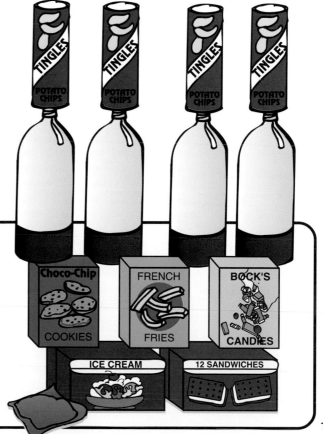

Plastic Bag Pyramid

Introduce the children to the food pyramid. Set up a model of the pyramid. Draw the outline of the pyramid on a large sheet of poster board. Attach quart-sized freezer bags to each of the six sections to represent a number in the range of servings per day suggested for each food group.

Bread, Cereal, Rice, and Pasta Group (6–11 servings)
Fruit Group (2–4 servings)
Vegetable Group (3–5 servings)
Milk, Yogurt, and Cheese Group (2–3 servings)
Meat, Poultry, Fish, Dried Beans, Eggs, and Nuts
   Group (2–3 servings)
Fats, Oils, and Sugars Group (use sparingly)

Mount the poster on a wall or bulletin board at a level accessible for the children in a center. Collect a number of food pictures for each of the groups. Have the children sort the pictures and place them in the bags. Because children often associate the top as best, you may need to turn the pyramid upside down to place sweets in the least favorable position.

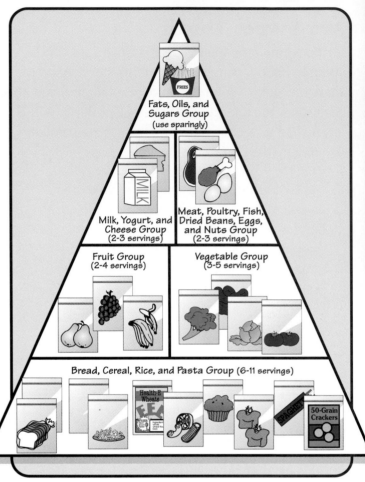

Pyramid Cut And Paste

Once children are familiar with the food pyramid and each of the six food groups, have them complete the activity on page 133.

SOCIAL STUDIES

Potluck Lunch

With the help of the cafeteria manager, plan a potluck lunch for your class. Take a tour of the school cafeteria to show the children what goes on behind the lunch counter. Have the cafeteria manager visit your classroom and discuss the process in preparing the school lunch. Have the manager help plan a menu suitable for the children to prepare and share in the classroom (English muffin pizzas, sliced fruit, milk, and ice cream). Have each child bring a designated food item to contribute to the meal. Prepare the meal as a class and enjoy a nutritious time together.

Field Trip

Contact a local pizza restaurant to arrange a field trip for your class. Have the staff give the children a tour of the restaurant facilities and demonstrate each of their jobs. Have them show the youngsters the steps to make a pizza. Stay and enjoy lunch.

Restaurant Play Center

Set up a play restaurant in a learning center. Place cups, plates, utensils, napkins, plastic food, menus, a notepad, and a pencil in the center. Have the children take turns playing the cook, waiter, and customers. Bon appétit!

ART

Bulletin Board

Bring a sub sandwich. Take it apart layer by layer as children observe. Have the children cooperatively make a giant sub sandwich from construction paper. Discuss the various food items and condiments that could be used in the sandwich: bread, ham, salami, tomatoes, onions, pickles, mayonnaise, mustard, etc. Have each child choose one food item and cut its shape from a large sheet of construction paper. Overlap the shapes slightly and glue them together to make a super sandwich. Cover a bulletin board with brightly colored paper or sponge paint the background paper to look like a tablecloth. Use large sheets of construction paper and have groups work together to make a plate, a napkin, a pickle spear, and a glass of milk with a straw. Attach the items to the bulletin board to create an attractive, mouth-watering display.

Placemats

Add a special touch to your class potluck lunch (see the activity on page 129). Have each child weave a placemat by using construction paper. Fold large sheets of construction paper in half. Cut slits, from the fold to 1 1/2 inches from the open edges, in the folded sheets one inch apart. Use a paper cutter to cut one-inch-wide strips from various colors of construction paper. In a learning center, have each child weave the strips in and out of the slits in the construction paper. She will create a beautiful paper placemat.

Fruit And Vegetable People

Have the children use their imaginations to create fruit and vegetable people. Use a variety of foods that can be easily pierced by toothpicks (potatoes, celery, apples, bell peppers, oranges, carrots, lemons, etc.). Have each child choose one fruit or vegetable for the body of the person. Give each child toothpicks and smaller food items (chives, lettuce leaves, raisins, sliced carrots, olives, etc.). Have each child create features for his fruit or vegetable person by securing smaller food items on the body with toothpicks.

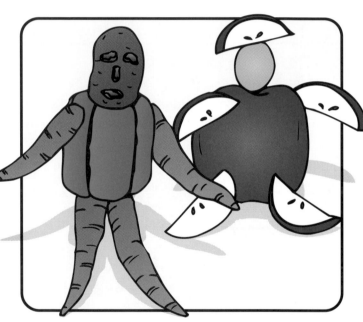

Fruit And Vegetable Printing

Cut a variety of fruits and vegetables in half to create a flat surface (apples, oranges, lemons, radishes, broccoli, celery, carrots, cauliflower, cabbages, etc.). Place the halves upside down on paper towels to drain. In a learning center place the drained food items, construction paper, and flat containers of tempera paint. Have each child select a sheet of construction paper and place it on a sheet of newspaper. Have him press a fruit or vegetable half into the paint and print onto the paper in a random fashion. Older children can use their imaginations to create an animal, a bowl of flowers, or a landscape. After the paint dries, frame each print by attaching it to a larger piece of poster board.

SNACK

CULMINATING ACTIVITY

Cabbage Soup

1 baking potato
2 individual stalks of celery
1 beet (or small can of sliced beets)
2 large tomatoes
a handful of pea pods (or frozen snow
    pea pods)
1 bell pepper
1 garlic clove
half a cabbage
1 cup brown rice
4–6 carrots
1 onion
a handful of fresh or frozen okra
salt
pepper

Precut the vegetables into strips. Invite the children to use plastic knives to chop the potato, celery, beet, bell pepper, carrots, and okra into bite-size pieces. Chop the tomato, onion, and cabbage. Encourage the children to taste any vegetables that are new to them. Add the rice, garlic, and pea pods; then cover with water. Add salt and pepper to taste. Cook this hearty cabbage soup on medium heat until the potatoes and carrots are soft. "Yummity Yum!"

Pyramid Snack

Have the children sit around tables in small groups. Then give each child a paper plate and place a container of each of the following foods in the center of the tables: goldfish crackers, pepperoni slices, cheese slices, carrot sticks, raisins, and candy corn. Review the food pyramid. Then have each child build his own pyramid snack. Ask him to select the foods that would go at each level of the food pyramid and place the food items in the correct order (see the example below).

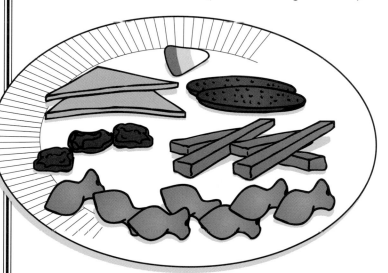

Name _____

Healthful Food   ## Junk Food

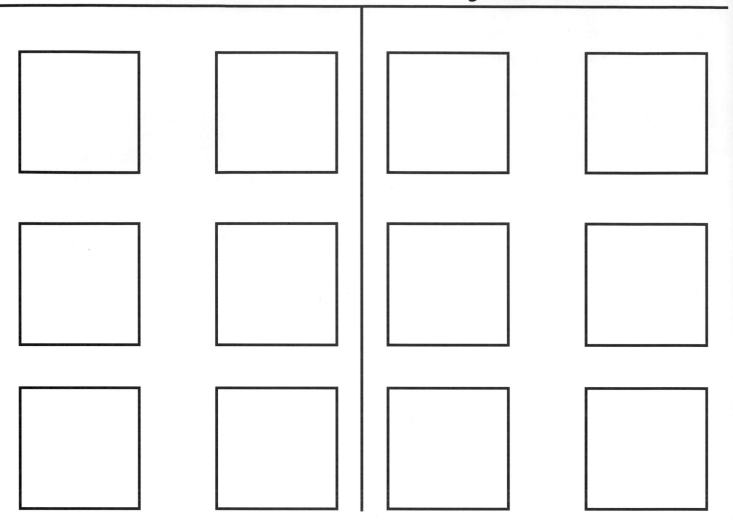

©The Education Center, Inc. • *Themes to Grow On* • *Fall & Winter* • TEC60799

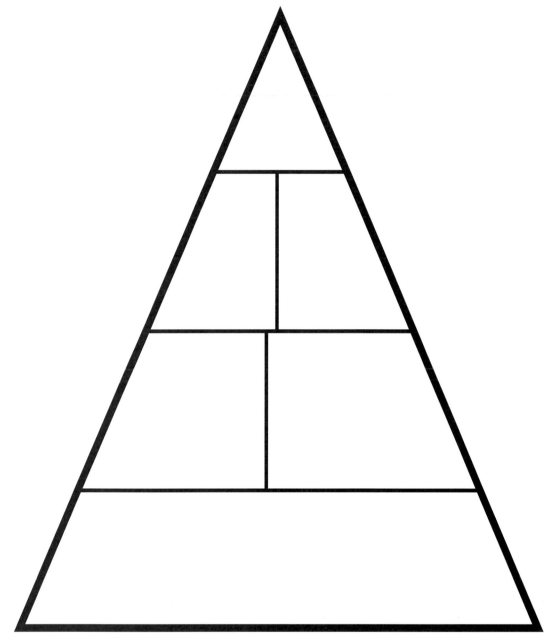

©The Education Center, Inc. • *Themes to Grow On* • *Fall & Winter* • TEC60799

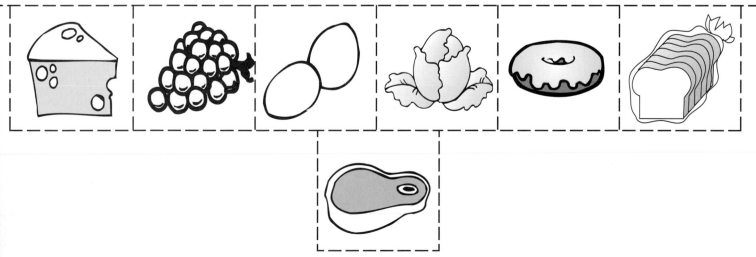

Use with "Pyramid Cut And Paste" on page 128.   133

Thanksgiving

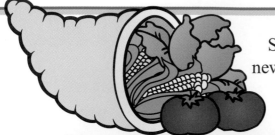

Sail with the Pilgrims on a sharing and caring journey to a new land, and discover the true meaning of Thanksgiving.

MATH

Thanksgiving Graphing

What better way to find out children's favorite Thanksgiving foods than by making a graph? Draw a grid on the chalkboard or on a large sheet of paper. Help the class think of three to five different foods that are usually eaten at Thanksgiving. After children decide their choices, place a picture of each food and write its name at the bottom of the grid. Have each child vote for her favorite food and color in the appropriate square on the grid. Discuss the results.

9					
8					
7					
6					
5					
4					
3					
2					
1					
	turkey	stuffing	potatoes	cran-berries	pie

Our Favorite Thanksgiving Foods

Pumpkin Pie Fractions

The children will enjoy learning more about fractions as they put together paper pumpkin pies. Cut five large circles from orange construction paper. Use a marker to divide the five pies respectively into halves, thirds, fourths, sixths, and eighths. Write the appropriate fraction on each piece. Laminate and cut apart the pie pieces on the marker lines. Mix up the slices and place them in a shoebox. Have the children in a learning center sort the slices and reassemble each of the pies.

Popcorn Patterning

Have the children create original patterns using colored popcorn. Pop the kernels in an air popper. To color the popped corn, place one tablespoon of dry tempera paint in a individual paper sandwich bag. Use one bag for each color. Place popcorn in each bag and shake. Pour the colored popcorn into individual containers. Have each child in a learning center make a color pattern by gluing the popcorn on a paper turkey feather.

Feather Patterning

Have small groups of children work together to create colorful paper turkeys. Divide the class into four groups. Give each group a large, brown turkey cutout, several sheets of bright-colored construction paper, feather patterns, scissors, glue, and pencils. Have each group use the feather patterns and construction paper to make tail feathers for the turkey. Have the group members work together to arrange the tail feathers in a pattern on the turkey shape. Check each of the patterns and have the children glue the feathers to the turkeys. Let the children use the paper scraps to make additional features on the turkey. When the turkeys are complete, attach each one to a separate sheet of construction paper or poster board, write each group member's name in the corner, and display the turkeys in the classroom or hallway.

Counting Order

To prepare for this activity, cut several popcorn shapes from poster board. Write a different numeral on each shape. Have the children stand or sit in a circle, and toss the popcorn shapes into the air. Let each shape fall to the floor. Have each child pick up one. Have the children arrange themselves in counting order according to the numerals printed on the popcorn shapes.

Numeral Recognition

To reinforce numeral recognition, have each child in a learning center make a simple math book. Use a marker to divide ten sheets of paper for each student in half horizontally. Bind each set of ten sheets between two construction-paper covers. Place pencils, numeral stencils for zero to nine, a stamp pad, and numeral stamps from zero to nine in a center. Give each child an empty book and have him trace a zero on the left-hand side of the first page with the stencil. Have him use the zero stamp to print zeros inside the traced numeral. On the right-hand side of the page, have him use the stamp to make a second zero. Have him repeat the same procedure for the numerals one to nine to complete the math book.

LANGUAGE ARTS

Letter Sounds

Cut several feather shapes from construction paper. Write a different letter on each feather. Place the feathers in a bag. Have the children take turns choosing a feather from the bag. Have each child name the letter and something for which he is thankful that begins with that letter. For example: *"B—I am thankful for birds."* Vary the activity by placing different-colored feathers in the bag. Have each child pull out a feather and name something for which he is thankful that is the same color. For example: "Blue—I am thankful for the sky."

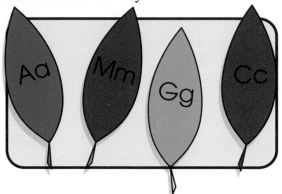

A Thanksgiving Rebus Story

Give each child in a small group a copy of the rebus booklet pages on pages 142 and 143. Read the rebus sentences to the group. Have the children read the sentences with you several times until each child in the group can read the sentences by himself. Have him cut apart the rebus pages and color the pictures. Bind the pages in order in a construction-paper cover to create a Thanksgiving book each child can read on his own.

Thanksgiving Spelling

Use the following activity to help children recognize several Thanksgiving words. Gather the following materials: a pocket chart, six to eight Thanksgiving pictures glued to tagboard squares, 3" x 1 1/2" tagboard letter cards, and plastic sandwich bags. In each sandwich bag, place a Thanksgiving picture with its name printed on the back and the letter cards needed to spell the picture's name.

Ask each child in a learning center to choose one sandwich bag, take the picture out of the bag, and look at the name printed on the back. Have him place the picture in the pocket chart and use the letters in the bag to spell the Thanksgiving word in the pocket chart beside the picture. Older children may then take the letters out of the chart, scramble them, and try to put them back in the correct order. Continue the activity until each child in the center has had a chance to spell all of the Thanksgiving words.

Language Experience

Read *Sarah Morton's Day: A Day In The Life Of A Pilgrim Girl* by Kate Waters to the children. Lead the children in a discussion of what a typical day in the life of a Pilgrim child was like. Have the children compare their daily chores and activities with those of the children long ago. Have them help you create a class book titled "Sarah Morton's Day: A Day In The Life Of An American Child." Have the children pretend that Sarah Morton is a member of their class and write a story about a day in the life of this fictional classmate. Begin by discussing the daily sequence of events in the life of a modern child. List the events on chart paper as they are described. In a small group setting, have each child choose one sentence from the chart, copy it on a sheet of paper, and illustrate it. Copy the sentence on the paper for a younger child. Bind the pages together to create a class book.

Creative Dramatics

Before introducing this activity to your class, cut several feather shapes from construction paper. Write a different task on each feather (picking berries, sewing, making butter, washing, gathering wood, fishing, setting animal traps, etc.). Lead the class in a discussion of the various tasks performed by Pilgrim and Native American children long ago. Have each child choose a feather, read the task, and act it out for her classmates. Ask the other children to guess which task is being performed. Repeat the activity until each child has had a turn.

Turkey Stuffing

Each child will enjoy "stuffing a turkey" as she participates in a game designed to reinforce vocabulary word recognition. To prepare this game, make a turkey bag for each child by attaching a turkey cutout to the front of a small paper lunch bag. Give each child a bag and place a stack of word cards in the center of the playing area. Have the children take turns drawing a card from the stack. If the child can read the word printed on her card, she may place it inside her turkey bag. If she is unable to read the word, she must place the card at the bottom of the stack. Play continues until all the word cards are used. Each child removes the cards from her bag and counts them. The player with the most cards wins. Vary the activity by using letter, number, or shape cards in place of word cards.

SCIENCE

Gross-Motor Development

Have the children participate in these traditional circle games/songs to enhance large-muscle control: "Skip To My Lou," "Looby Lou," "Farmer In The Dell," and "The Old Brass Wagon."

Turkey Toss

Attach a picture of a turkey to one side of a brown lunch bag and stuff it with newspaper. Staple the bag shut and hang it by a string from a chart stand. Place a strip of masking tape on the floor four feet from the chart stand. Have each child stand behind the tape line and try to hit the turkey using a beanbag or soft ball designed for indoor play. Give each child three tries to hit the turkey.

Preserving Foods

Discuss the many ways we use to preserve foods today. Show the children examples of foods preserved by each of the following methods:

refrigeration—an orange
freezing—a frozen dinner
drying—raisins
canning—a can of corn
pasteurization—milk
adding sugar—jelly
adding salt and vinegar—pickles

Describe some of the methods the Pilgrims used to preserve their foods:

drying on a cloth in the sun—corn, peas, beans, wheat
salting and smoking—pork and fish
storing in cloth bags or barrels—apples and potatoes

Use this apple butter recipe to allow the children to participate in a way to preserve apples.

Quick Apple Butter

Combine five cups of applesauce, six cups of sugar, and one small box of wild strawberry Jell-O. Cook the mixture in a heavy iron pot for ten minutes, stirring constantly. Add ground cinnamon to taste. Serve it on bread.

SOCIAL STUDIES

The *Mayflower*

After reading ...*If You Sailed On The Mayflower* by Ann McGovern, let your class experience its very own *Mayflower* adventure. Draw a 106-by-25-foot space on the playground using chalk. With the help of as many other classes as needed, have approximately 130 children stand inside the space. Explain that the space is the same size as the deck of the *Mayflower*. Help the children experience the crowded conditions by staying inside the space for five minutes. Take a photograph of the group or videotape the activity to watch at a later time.

Packing Belongings

Each family on the *Mayflower* could take a chest for clothes and other belongings. The men brought their guns, swords, and tools. The women brought the things they needed for cooking and the family Bible. Belongings that did not fit in the chest had to be left behind.

Let your children pretend to be Pilgrims preparing to sail on the *Mayflower*. Send home with each child a grocery bag and a note asking that she pack the things she would take to the new land inside the bag. Then, on a designated day, have each child share the belongings she packed with her classmates.

Squanto

Discuss how Squanto was a friend to the Pilgrims. Next have the children define the word *friend*. Ask each child to think of a way he is a helpful friend to others. Have him draw a picture of himself involved in the helping activity. Finally have each child share his drawing with the class.

ART

Table Decorations

Before the class Thanksgiving meal (see page 141), have the children make napkin rings and place cards to use as table decorations. Place glue, markers or crayons, dried beans, Indian corn kernels, paper-towel rolls cut into one-inch sections, and 3" x 5" cardboard strips in a learning center. Have each child make a napkin ring by gluing dried beans and corn kernels in rows around a paper-towel roll section. Then have him create a place card by first writing his name in the center of a cardboard strip. Have him glue dried beans and corn kernels around the top edge of the card. Complete the place card by having him push the bottom edge of the card into a small strip of clay and then pressing acorns into the clay.

Torn-Paper Cornucopia

To form the cornucopia horn, glue jute twine to construction paper in the shape of a horn. Have the children fill in the horn with different shades of torn brown construction paper. After the glue dries, cut out the horn and attach it to a large sheet of poster board. Have each child make a piece of fruit or a vegetable by tearing, instead of cutting, bright-colored construction paper. Glue the torn foods to the open end of the horn and use a marker to add details. Display the cornucopia on a door or small bulletin board.

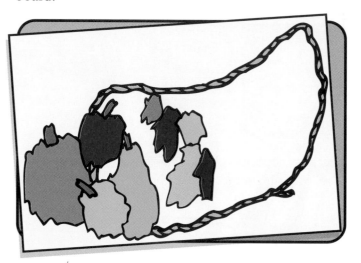

Bulletin Board

Children will love creating this unique turkey for an attractive bulletin-board display. Cut out a turkey feather from tagboard for each child in the classroom. For homework, have the children decorate the tagboard feathers any way they wish. Cut a large turkey shape from brown paper and attach it to a bulletin board. Add features such as eyes, feet, a wattle, and a beak to the turkey. Arrange the children's feathers around the turkey's body.

140

SNACK

Pumpkin Muffins

3 cups Bisquick baking mix
2 eggs
2/3 cup sugar
1/2 cup milk
1 cup canned pumpkin
1 teaspoon ground cinnamon
1 teaspoon ground nutmeg
1/2 teaspoon ground cloves

Mix all ingredients until moistened. Stir vigorously for 30 seconds. Pour the batter into greased muffin tins. Bake at 375° for 16 to 18 minutes. Cool for 10 minutes and remove the muffins from the pan. Makes 12 to 15 large muffins.

CULMINATING ACTIVITY

Thanksgiving Meal

Read *Stone Soup* by Marcia Brown to the children. Discuss how a good soup was made when everyone helped bring the ingredients. Ask the children if they would like to participate in making Stone Soup for their school's Thanksgiving meal. Discuss the various ingredients that will be needed. Assign each child an item to bring for the soup or one of the additional items needed to make the meal complete.

The day before the Thanksgiving meal is to be eaten, plan a time in the morning when the soup can be made. Ask several parent volunteers to come in and help with the preparation. Divide the class into small groups with a parent supervisor for each group. Give each child in a group a raw vegetable to peel and cut into small pieces. Plastic serrated knives can be used to cut most of the vegetables. Rinse the raw vegetables after cutting. Have the children take turns putting the Stone Soup ingredients into Crockpots. Let the soup cook all day and all night. The next day serve the soup with the other food items and enjoy a delicious Thanksgiving meal.

Stone Soup
tomato juice
celery
potatoes
cabbage
Veg-All
onions
ground beef

Additional Items
paper plates
Styrofoam bowls
plastic spoons
paper cups
crackers
seedless grapes

popcorn
apple juice
pumpkin muffins (see the recipe on this page)
plastic serrated knives

Thanksgiving
Rebus Booklet

Use with "A Thanksgiving Rebus Story" on page 136.

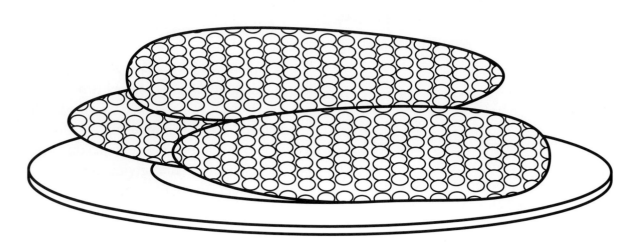

A will bring .

1

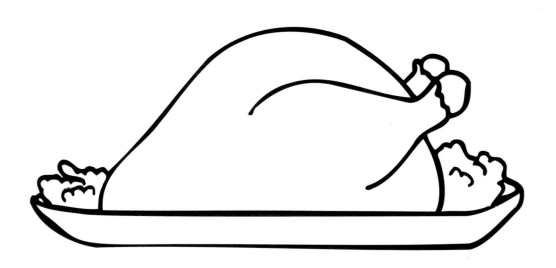

A will bring a .

2

©The Education Center, Inc. • *Themes to Grow On* • *Fall & Winter* • TEC60799

A  will bring  .

3

A , , and  will eat a feast.

4

Winter Festival

Traditions and holidays come alive during this festive winter season with ideas and activities designed to make your class more aware of cultural celebrations.

MATH

Graphing

Have each child tell you what he thinks makes Rudolph the reindeer fly. List the ideas on chart paper. Prepare a graph using four or five of the responses. Have each child place a holiday sticker beside his favorite reason. Discuss which reason received the most votes, which received the least votes, and why each received the votes it did.

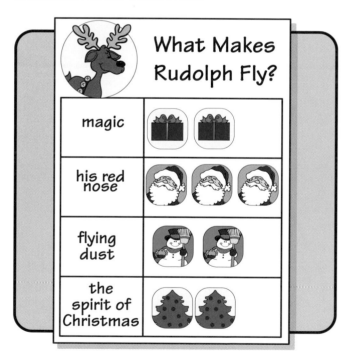

Candy Estimation

Fill a plastic bag with Christmas candy. Have each child estimate how many pieces of candy are in the bag. Have her write her name and estimate on a slip of paper. Collect the slips of paper. Count out the candy in groups of ten in individual cups. Determine whose estimate came closest to the actual number.

Card Sorting And Counting

Have the children bring in old Christmas cards. Place the cards in a large box. Have the children in a learning center classify the cards (cards with pictures of Santa, winter scenes, words only, etc.). Then have each child count the cards in each group.

Visual Memory

Collect several small, cleaned milk cartons and pairs of holiday items (candy canes, bows, ornaments, etc.). Cut the top off each carton. Wrap the bottom portion of each carton in holiday paper. Place one item under each carton. Have the children in a learning center try to locate identical items by lifting two cartons at a time. Have the children take turns and replace the cartons once they have looked under them. A child who finds two matching objects may keep them until the game ends. Replace the items under the cartons with two new matching items.

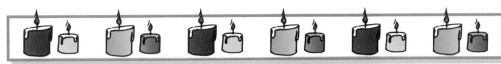

Reindeer Story Problems

Have the children listen carefully to each reindeer story problem. Have them answer by holding up the correct number of fingers or numeral card.

Once there were three reindeer getting ready to pull Santa's sleigh. They started to pull, but the sleigh was too heavy. Three more reindeer came to help. How many reindeer in all were pulling Santa's sleigh? *(6)*

Dasher, Dancer, Prancer, and Vixen were getting ready for Christmas Eve. Comet, Cupid, Donner, and Blitzen joined them. How many reindeer in all were getting ready for Christmas Eve? *(8)*

Santa took eight of his reindeer for a practice flight. Four of them became sick and had to stop. How many reindeer were left to fly with Santa? *(4)*

It was the day after Christmas. Dasher, Dancer, Prancer, Vixen, Comet, Cupid, Donner, Blitzen, and Rudolph were getting ready for a nap. Mrs. Claus gave each of them a snack. Four of the reindeer went to sleep. How many of the reindeer were still awake? *(5)*

Santa's elves need to put bells on the reindeer for the Christmas Eve journey. They found four reindeer in the stable and three on the roof. How many reindeer did the elves find? *(7)*

Countdown Santa

Duplicate the counting grid (page 152) on red construction paper for each child. Duplicate the Santa hat pattern on page 153 to make cardboard patterns for tracers. Have each child trace Santa's hat on red construction paper. Duplicate Santa's head on pink construction paper. Have each child cut out the hat and head. Have him use paper scraps to make a nose and two eyes. Have him cut out the counting grid and glue it to the head at the dotted line. Have him glue the eyes, nose, and hat to the head. Glue cotton balls to the hat to create fur and to the head to make Santa's hair and mustache. Each child can take his Santa home along with a parent letter (see below) and glue a cotton ball on the counting grid each of the 24 days before Santa arrives.

Dear Parent,
   Count down from 24 to 1.
Each day (starting on December 1), help your child glue a cotton ball to the next numeral on Santa's beard.

   Thank you,

   _____
   (teacher)

145

LANGUAGE ARTS

Holiday Letter Boxes

Remove the tops from five large gift boxes. Cover the boxes with holiday wrapping paper. Attach an alphabet letter to the side of each box using tape or Velcro so the letter can be easily changed. Collect several small items from the classroom that begin with the letters that are on the five boxes. Place the items in a large holiday shopping bag. Have the children in a learning center take the objects from the shopping bag and place them in the box displaying the corresponding initial consonant sound.

Letter Recognition

Draw the outline of a large Christmas tree on a chalkboard. Draw several circles on the tree to represent ornaments. Write a letter in each circle. Have each child in a small group name a letter. If she names the letter correctly, she may erase the letter and the circle. The game ends when all of the circles have been erased. Vary the activity using vocabulary words, blends, or numerals in the circles.

Festive Writing

Help each child in a learning center make a holiday book he can write and read independently. Write several holiday words (such as *bow, candle, tree, star, bell, stocking,* etc.) on individual cards. Illustrate each word by drawing or pasting a picture on each card. Laminate the cards. Print the sentence, "I like a _____," at the bottom of a sheet of paper. Duplicate a quantity of this sheet to make pages for each book. Print the title "Things I Like During The Holidays" on the front of large sheets of folded construction paper. Place the cards, book pages, book covers, crayons, and pencils in a learning center. Have each child in the center choose a card and copy the word in the blank on a book page. Have her draw a picture of that object above the sentence. Have her complete several pages. Staple them inside a cover to make an individual holiday book.

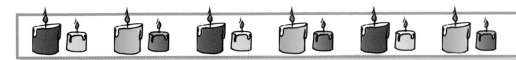

Brainstorming

Read and discuss *Alexander And The Wind-Up Mouse* by Leo Lionni. Then ask the class to describe what Annie, the owner of the wind-up mouse, planned to do with her unwanted toys after her birthday party. Next have the children think of other ways Annie could have disposed of her toys (sold them at a yard sale, donated them to a charity, given them to a needy child, etc.). Finally place a box for unwanted toys in the classroom. Tell the children they may bring unwanted toys from home and place them in the box. Then take the box of toys to Goodwill or another charitable organization.

A Needy Language Experience

Later in the week, review the lesson on *wants* and *needs*. Have the children think of things they would like to save their money to buy. Make a list of the items on a sheet of chart paper. Place this list beside the lists of needs and wants in a learning center. Give each child three sheets of paper and have her label them "Needs," "Wants," and "Save For." Have her draw three things she needs on the first page, three things she wants on the second page, and one thing she would like to save for on the last page. Bind the pages together to create an individual book.

Needs And Wants

Read the book *Claude The Dog: A Christmas Story* by Dick Gackenbach. Discuss how Claude demonstrated generosity and compassion by giving all of his holiday gifts to a homeless dog. Discuss the differences between *needs* and *wants*. Help the children make a list of things that they need and a list of things they want. Explain to your children that homeless children do not have many of the things they need or want. Ask the children if they would like to help a homeless or needy child. Send a note home and ask parents to send in small, inexpensive items (toothbrush, socks, mittens, crayons, hats) that could be donated. Decorate a large box and place it in the room. Have the children place their donated items in the box. Arrange to take the items to a shelter or an agency that helps the needy.

SCIENCE

Evergreen Trees

Arrange a time with the local forestry department for a representative to come to your class and talk about the characteristics of evergreen trees. Take the class on a nature walk around the school grounds to look for evergreens.

SOCIAL STUDIES

Edible Christmas Candles

Christmas is a Christian celebration of the birth of Jesus. Candles in homes during ancient times and today represent a feeling of hope and goodness which prevails throughout the season. Follow the directions and have the children assemble an edible fruit candle.

Fruit Candle

1 pineapple ring
1/2 banana
1 cherry
1 toothpick
1 small paper plate

Place the pineapple ring on a small paper plate. Set the half of a banana in the hole of the pineapple. Insert a toothpick in the cherry and push the other end through the top of the banana.

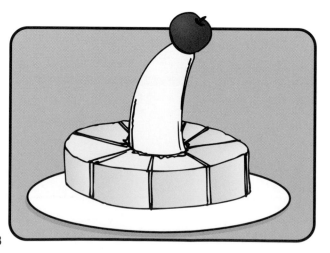

Hanukkah

Hanukkah is a Jewish festival that lasts for eight days and is based on an ancient event. Judah Maccabee led the Jewish people in a victory over the Syrians. The Jewish people wanted to celebrate by lighting a lamp to rededicate the temple. However, the people could only find enough oil to burn the lamp for one day. Amazingly, the oil lasted for eight days.

The *menorah* is a candlestick that holds nine candles. Eight candles represent the eight days that the lamp burned. The *shammash* or "helper" candle is used to light the other candles. Each night of Hanukkah, Jewish families gather to light a candle on the menorah and share special foods, songs, games, and gifts. *Latkes,* potato pancakes served at least once during Hanukkah, can be made using this recipe.

Latkes

2 cups grated potatoes
1 small onion
1 teaspoon salt
1/4 teaspoon pepper
1 tablespoon flour
1/2 teaspoon baking powder
2 eggs, well-beaten
Oil
Applesauce

Peel the potatoes and soak them in cold water. Drain the potatoes and grate. Grate the onion and mix it with potatoes. Add salt and pepper. Mix in the flour and baking powder. Add the eggs. Drop the mixture by teaspoons into a hot, well-greased frying pan. Flatten latkes with the back of a spoon. Brown both sides. Drain on paper towels. Serve latkes with applesauce.

Kwanzaa

Kwanzaa is a holiday observed by some African-Americans in celebration of the African harvest. It is also a time for African-Americans to honor their ancestors and celebrate the joys of family. Kwanzaa begins on December 26 and ends on January 1. On each of the seven days, families gather to light a candle, discuss one of the seven principles of black culture, and exchange homemade gifts. To help the children understand Kwanzaa's focus on the harvest, have each child bring a fruit or vegetable from home. Place the food in a decorated box and donate the food box to a needy family.

Las Posadas

Mexican-Americans celebrate Las Posadas during the Christmas season. Each night from December 16 to December 24, friends and neighbors gather to form a parade and act out Mary and Joseph's search for a *posada,* or inn. Two children assume the roles of Mary and Joseph and lead the parade from house to house. On the final night, the parade reaches a designated destination and a tiny figure of Baby Jesus is placed in a manger scene. In south-central Texas some cities line the streets with luminaries during the Las Posadas celebration. Have each child make a luminary to take home for the holidays. Give each child a white paper sack. Have him decorate the bag and fill it with one to two inches of sand. Ask parents to push a tea candle into the center of the sand.

ART

Gift Tags

Collect old holiday cards. Cut the back off each one and use a hole puncher to punch holes around the outside edges of the cards. Have each child in a small group choose one of the cards and use a piece of yarn to lace around it. Secure the ends of the yarn by tying them together. Have each child address the card, wrap her cinnamon ornament (see page 151) or other gift in tissue paper, and place it in a white paper bag. Fold the top of the bag down, punch two holes in the top, and lace a piece of yarn through the two holes. Tie the gift tag to the bag.

Bulletin Board

After reading aloud *The Polar Express* by Chris Van Allsburg, have the children create a magical train ride across a large bulletin board in the classroom. Cover the top half of the board with light blue paper. Cover the bottom with white. Use construction paper to make a railroad track that winds its way through the snow. Have a group of children make houses, shops, trees, and small animals from scraps of brightly colored construction paper. Staple these around the railroad tracks. Have another group make a train. Give the children construction paper and several shape patterns. Have them trace the shapes, cut them out, and assemble them to make a locomotive and several boxcars. Staple the train to the track. Add cotton snow to the tops of the buildings and star stickers to the sky.

Gingerbread Houses

Have the children or parents bring in the materials needed for the houses. Collect a small milk carton for each child in the classroom. Rinse the inside of each carton, let it dry, and staple the top closed. Mix various small candies such as gumdrops, M&M's, and Skittles together in a bowl and place them in a learning center. Give each child in the center a milk carton, several graham crackers, a small bowl of icing (recipe below), and a craft stick. Have him spread the icing on the backs of the graham crackers with the craft stick. Attach the crackers to the milk carton to create the walls and roof of the gingerbread house. Encourage the children to work quickly because the graham crackers get soggy. Have each child attach the candy to the house with the remaining icing.

Icing

1 egg white
1 1/2 cups 10X confectioners' sugar
1/2 teaspoon cream of tartar

Beat the egg white for a short time. Gradually add the sugar and cream of tartar. Continue to beat until the mixture becomes smooth. To delay icing from hardening, keep the bowl covered with a damp cloth or plastic wrap. (This makes enough icing for two houses.)

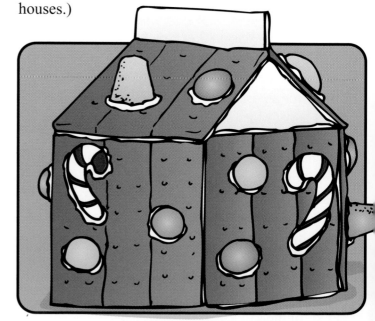

SNACK

Holiday Cider

1 gallon apple cider or apple juice
1 cup Red-Hots (cinnamon candies)
1 cinnamon stick per child

Pour the cider into a saucepan. Add the candies. Heat and stir the cider until the candies melt. Pour it into individual cups, allow to cool slightly, and serve each cup with a cinnamon stick. This makes approximately 24 servings.

CULMINATING ACTIVITY

Cinnamon Ornament

Make ornaments using cinnamon and applesauce and fill your classroom with the wonderful smell of the holiday season.

To make 12 small ornaments use:
3 3/4 oz. ground cinnamon
1/2 cup applesauce

Mix the cinnamon and applesauce until the mixture is the consistency of cookie dough. Roll the dough between two sheets of waxed paper. Have each child use a small cookie cutter to cut out an ornament. Use a drinking straw to punch a hole in the top of each ornament. Allow ornaments to dry about 36 hours, turning them occasionally. Thread a piece of ribbon through the hole in each ornament and tie it to make a hanger. The ornaments may be given to family members or friends.

Winter Festival
Santa's beard/counting grid
Use with "Countdown Santa" on page 145.

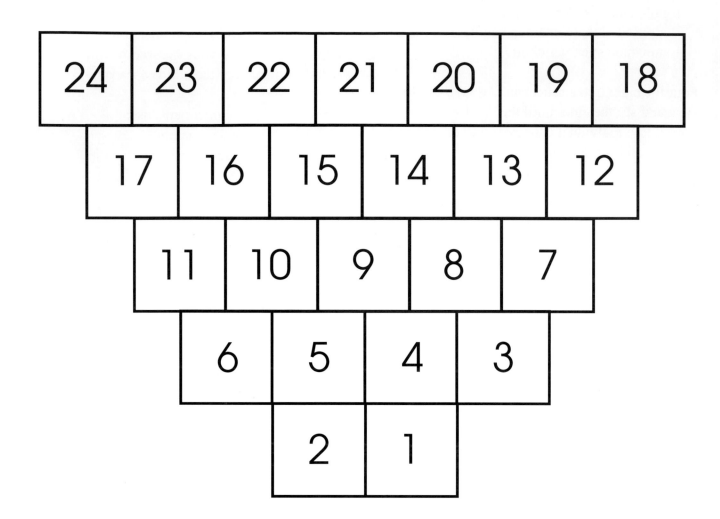

©The Education Center, Inc. • *Themes to Grow On* • *Fall & Winter* • TEC60799

head

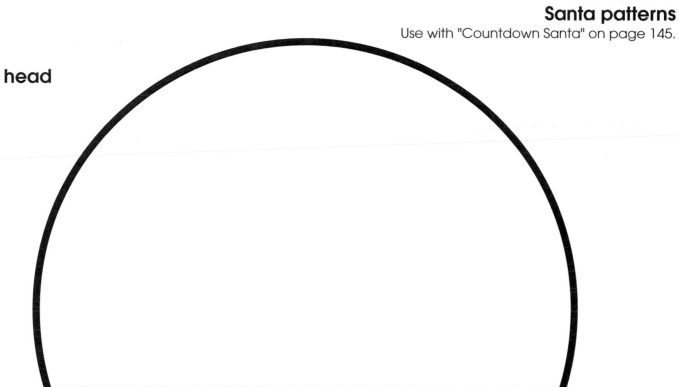

Glue the counting grid here.

hat

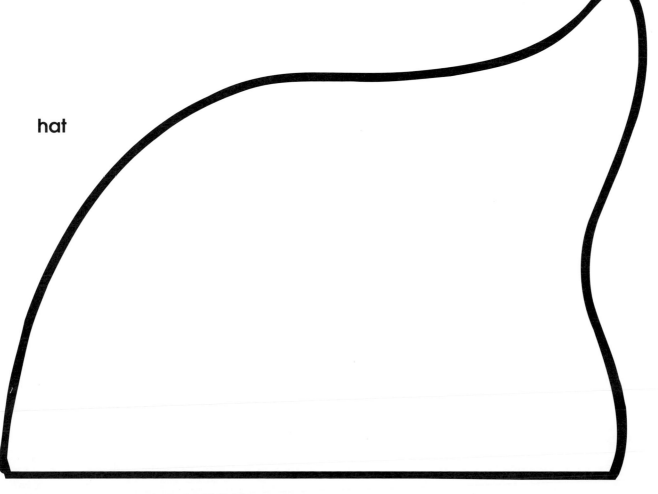

 # Transportation

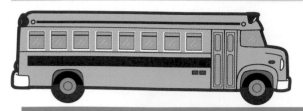

All aboard the Transportation Express! Let your imaginations soar to destinations unknown as you travel by land, water, and air.

MATH

Traveling To School

Make a graph showing how the children get to school. Draw a grid on a chalkboard or large sheet of paper. Label each row by drawing or attaching a picture of a bus, car, bike, or child walking. Have the children tell how they arrive at school and graph their responses. Discuss the results.

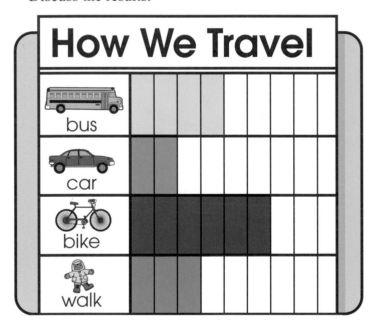

And They're Off!

Place several small cars and a set of wooden building blocks in a learning center. Have the children use the blocks to build a racetrack on a slick surface such as a tile floor or table. Have each child choose a car and race it with the others down the track. Ask the children to decide which car came in first, second, and third. After several races, have the children build a new track, choose a different car, and have additional races.

Types Of Transportation

Have each child bring in up to three transportation toys from home. Ask each child to put his name on his toys before bringing them to school to avoid any confusion over ownership. Place all of the toys in a box and encourage the children to think of ways to sort them into different groups such as by color, size, mode of transportation, etc. Then have your youngsters sort the vehicles. Vary the activity by asking the children to line up the toys by size from smallest to largest.

Figure It Out

Have youngsters solve word problems using the vehicles that the children brought from home for "Types Of Transportation" on page 154. Some examples include:

1. Alan has 2 cars and 1 truck. How many vehicles does Alan have altogether? *(3)*
2. Bryan has 1 car and 2 trucks. Patrick has 2 cars and 1 truck. How many cars do the boys have altogether? *(3)* How many trucks do the boys have altogether? *(3)* How many vehicles are there in all? *(6)*
3. Brenda had 1 boat and 2 airplanes. She gave 1 airplane to Angie. How many vehicles does Brenda have now? *(2)*
4. The boys have 5 motorcycles and 5 bicycles. The girls have 5 cars and 5 helicopters. How many vehicles are there in all? *(20)*

A Long Flight

Have each child use an 8 1/2" x 11" sheet of paper to make a paper airplane. Demonstrate each of the following directions, stopping after each step to check the children's work. When the airplanes are complete, have small groups of children fly their airplanes from a designated place in the classroom. Visually measure to see which plane flew the greatest distance. Then take the children outside. Have them line up, listen for a signal, and fly their airplanes. Measure the greatest distance again.

Directions for making the airplane:

1. Fold the paper in half vertically.
2. Unfold the paper and hold it vertically. Fold the top right and left corners in to the middle so they touch the crease.
3. Refold the paper so that the folded corners meet. Position the paper horizontally on the table with the fold nearest you.
4. From the point, fold one side halfway to the bottom crease.
5. Fold again, matching the edges, to the crease.
6. Turn it over and repeat steps 4 and 5 on the other side.

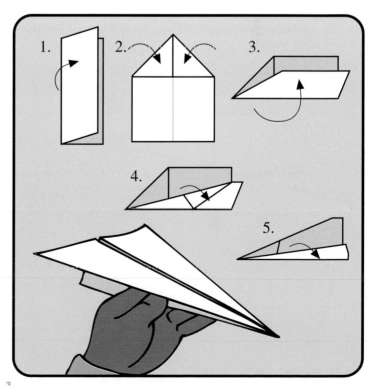

LANGUAGE ARTS

Following Directions

Give each child crayons and a copy of the reproducible on page 162. Read the story below. Each time a color word is read, have children color over the appropriate dotted lines in the pictures using that color of crayon.

Sarah was so excited! She was going to Walt Disney World with her family on vacation. She picked up her red-striped suitcase and went outside. The bright, yellow sun was shining. Her dad was packing the family van. The van was white with green stripes. Sarah handed the suitcase to Dad and he put it in the back of the van with the other things needed for the long trip. Suddenly the sky became dark and blue raindrops began to fall. Dad quickly packed the last of the luggage while the others got into the van.

Then the family started down the road toward the airport. In a few short minutes, Sarah saw the enormous brick building in the distance. Jets were taking off and landing on the runways nearby. Dad parked the van and got out the luggage. Sarah and the rest of her family went inside the terminal to wait. Sarah looked out the huge glass window and saw their plane. It had orange stripes on the tail and nose of the plane. It also has purple edges around the passengers' windows. Sarah could hardly wait to board the beautiful plane and begin the trip to Walt Disney World.

Cable Car Events

After reading aloud *Maybelle The Cable Car* by Virginia Lee Burton, give each child a copy of the pattern on page 163. Have her use colored pencils to draw clues about three main events on the strip as they appeared in the story. Then ask her to color the picture of the cable car. Have her cut out the pattern and sequencing strip. Use an X-acto knife to cut along the dotted lines on the cable car. Ask each child to insert the strip through the two slits to form a tachistoscope. She can then use the cable car and the strip to retell the story to a friend.

Vocabulary Word Recognition

Help the children learn the familiar song lyrics "A Peanut Sat on a Railroad Track". Create an interactive chart by copying the poem on a sheet of chart paper, omitting the following words: *peanut, railroad, track, heart, a-flutter, five-fifteen,* and *peanut butter.* Write each of the omitted words on a separate strip of paper. Draw a picture clue for each word on the back of the strip. Laminate the chart paper and the paper strips. Attach one-half of a Velcro circle to the back of each strip and the other half to the space on the chart where the word belongs. Have the children in a learning center use the picture clues on the backs of the strips to place the missing words in the correct spaces on the chart. Encourage each child in the group to read the poem.

Alphabet Train

The children in your classroom will enjoy working together to make an alphabet train of beginning sounds. Give each child a 9" x 12" sheet of construction paper, a scrap of black paper, and a small circle tracer. Ask her to use the black paper and the circle tracer to make two wheels. Have her glue the wheels to a long strip of the construction paper to create a car for the alphabet train. Assign each child a letter and have her look through an old magazine to find a picture or pictures that begin with that letter's sound. Have her cut out the pictures and glue them to the appropriate alphabet car. Make an engine and any extra cars needed to complete the train. Mount the alphabet train on a wall in the classroom.

Three Of A Kind

Park a tricycle in your classroom. Ask the children to look at the tricycle carefully and name each of its parts. Have the children name three parts they see that are the same. Have the children name other things that have three parts that are the same or similar: a triangle, rings in a circus, a traffic light, *The Three Little Pigs.* List the responses on chart paper. Let each child make his own "Three Book." Cut the front and back covers and three pages in the shape of a triangle and staple them together. Have him select three things from the chart and draw one on each page of the book. Label each illustration with the corresponding words or have the child copy the words from the chart.

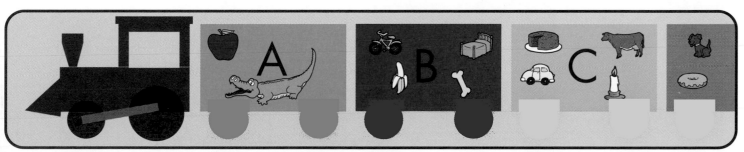

SCIENCE

Build A Vehicle

Place various building materials in a learning center, such as Legos and Flexiblocks. Have the children in the center use the materials to create different types of vehicles. Allow children to decide whether to work together to build one large vehicle or to work independently to create individual vehicles.

Wheels

Place a supply of wooden building blocks in a cardboard box. Have a volunteer help you with an experiment to determine the easiest way to move the box of blocks. Have the volunteer pick up the box and move it to another place in the classroom. Have him put the box on the floor and pull it to another location. Next have him push the box back to its original spot. Finally place the box in a wagon and have the child pull it across the room. Ask him which method of moving the box was the easiest. Ask him why he thought that method made moving the box easier. Have other volunteers repeat the experiment to see if they agree.

Inclined Plane

Use an inclined plane to demonstrate how different variables affect the movement of vehicles. Roll two similar cars down the inclined plane: one with wheels and one without. Discuss the advantages that wheels provide. Then race several vehicles of varying sizes and weights down the inclined plane and compare the results. Discuss how the size and weight of each vehicle affect its performance. Next change the surface of the inclined plane and compare the rate at which a vehicle travels on each surface. Suggested surfaces include thick carpet, plastic, corrugated cardboard, a bath towel, and sandpaper. Finally vary the incline of the plane before rolling a car down its surface. Discuss how the amount of incline determines the speed at which the car travels down the plane.

SOCIAL STUDIES

Field Trip

Organize a field trip to one of several locations to enhance children's understanding of various modes of transportation. Places might include an airport, a railroad station, or a city bus depot. When appropriate, include a tour and/or a ride on the featured mode of transportation.

Dramatic Play

Set up a dramatic play center in the classroom where children can pretend to be riding a bus, boarding an airplane, traveling by train, or sailing on a ship. Place a props box in the center complete with a roll of tickets, a hole puncher, a memo pad, a pencil, play money, a jacket, a variety of hats, magazines, a tray of play food, luggage, and several chairs.

Maps

Show the children a variety of maps and point out the unique features of each one. Discuss how the people who live in the various places pictured on the maps travel from one place to another. Have the children help you create a map of how they travel to school. On a large bulletin board, construct a map of the school and the surrounding streets. Label the school and the streets. Point out where each child lives on the map. Have him make his house from construction paper. Place the house on the street where the child lives and label it with the child's name. Discuss how each child travels to school. Have the children make paper buses, cars, and walking children to add to the map. Attach the graph created in "Traveling To School" on page 154 to one of the corners of or right beside the bulletin board.

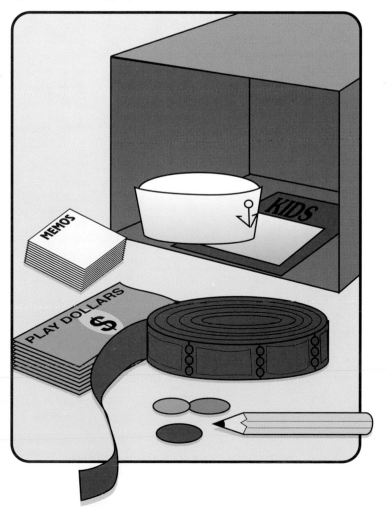

ART

Box Vehicles

Have each child bring a large cardboard box from home. Cut the flaps off the top of the box. Cut a hole in the bottom of the box large enough to slip it over a child's waist. Let each child use bright-colored tempera paints to paint her box. When the paint dries, attach large painted paper plates to the sides of the box to make wheels. Let each child use scissors, glue, markers, and construction-paper scraps to make additional features for her vehicle, such as headlights, a license plate, a horn, numbers, and stripes. Punch a hole in opposite sides of the top edge of the box and thread a piece of cord through each of the holes. Have the child hold her cardboard vehicle up around her waist and tie the cord behind her neck.

Nametags

Have each child make a nametag to wear on a transportation field trip. (See "Field Trip" on page 159.) Cut old maps into several small squares. Give each child one of the map squares, a larger square of construction paper, glue, scissors, and a marker. Have him cut the shape of a vehicle from the map square and glue it to the construction-paper square. Have him use the marker and write his name under the vehicle. Laminate each nametag. Hot glue two buttons on the vehicle for wheels. Punch a hole in the top of the nametag and thread a long piece of yarn through it. Have each child wear the nametag around his neck like a necklace.

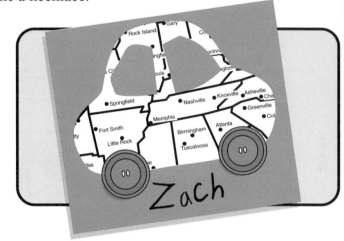

Shape Collage

After reading several books about various types of vehicles, set up a learning center in the classroom where children can make shape collages of their favorite vehicles. Place construction paper, paper scraps, scissors, glue, and shape patterns in the center. Have each child use the paper scraps and the patterns to create his vehicle. Have him glue the vehicle on a construction-paper background and use the remaining paper scraps to make any additional features such as roads, stop signs, trees, clouds, or traffic lights. Vary the activity by having each child write a sentence about his vehicle on the collage. Bind all of the pages together with a cover to create a class book.

Transportation

SNACK

Egg Boats

1 egg for every 2 children
mayonnaise
mustard
salt
pepper
1 slice of cheese for every 4 children
toothpicks

To create the egg boat hulls, hard-boil the eggs and peel them. Cut the eggs in half. Remove the yolks and mix them with mayonnaise, mustard, salt, and pepper. Spoon a small amount of the egg mixture into each egg half. Then cut sliced cheese into quarters to make the boat sails. Push a toothpick through each piece of cheese and insert it into the egg white.

CULMINATING ACTIVITY

After each child has completed his box vehicle (see "Box Vehicles" on page 160), schedule a time for a vehicle parade. Let each child put on his vehicle, get in line with his classmates, and parade throughout the school. To add interest to the parade, let children use horns, kazoos, or other musical instruments.

Following directions, colors

Name _____

162

©The Education Center, Inc. • *Themes to Grow On • Fall & Winter* • TEC60799

Use with "Following Directions" on page 156.

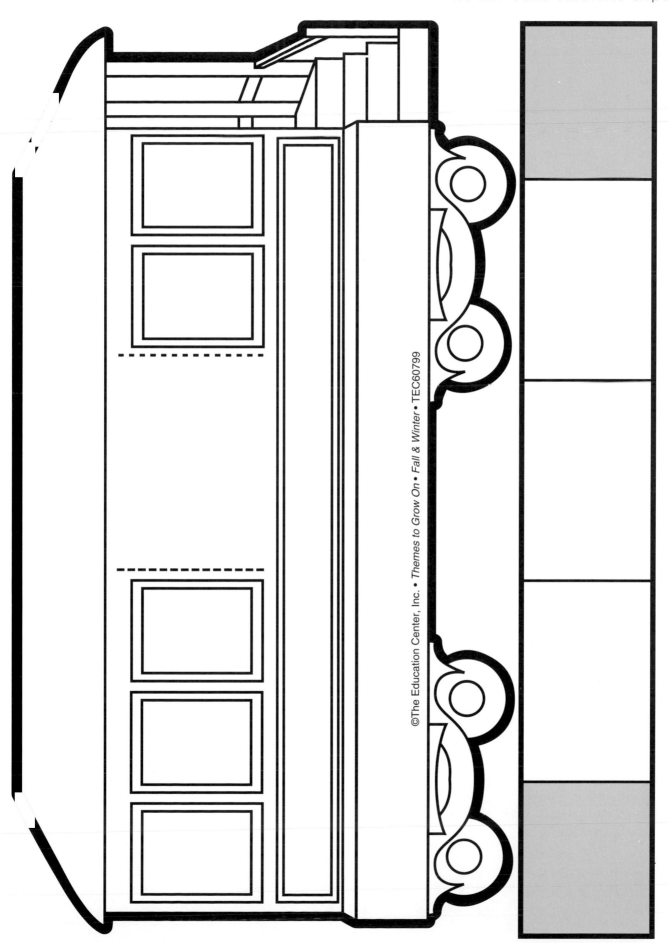

©The Education Center, Inc. • *Themes to Grow On* • *Fall & Winter* • TEC60799

Polar Animals

Travel the icy waters to the ends of the earth in your exploration of polar animals and their habitats.

MATH

Time

The puffin is an odd-looking bird that lives in the Arctic waters of the Atlantic and Pacific oceans. Puffins are excellent swimmers and divers. They can also flap their wings 350 times a minute. Share this information with the children in a small group. Review how many seconds are in a minute. Then let each child discover how many times in one minute he can repeat a certain activity such as the following:

- Toss a ball or beanbag into the air and catch it.
- Jump with both feet together over a rolled-up piece of newspaper that is held six to ten inches above the floor.
- Have pairs of children toss a ball back and forth. The ball must be caught each time or the child needs to start over.

While one child or pair performs an activity, have the other children count the number of repetitions per minute. Time each child or pair using a stopwatch, minute timer, or second hand on a clock.

Polar Bear Subtraction

Ask each child in a small group to pretend to be a hungry polar bear that wants some fish to eat. Give her a napkin and a cup filled with ten goldfish crackers. Ask her to use the fish crackers to show what happens in this story problem. Have each child spread out her crackers on a napkin. Each time the bear in the story eats fish, have her eat that many crackers.

One morning a polar bear caught ten fish. He ate two fish for breakfast and saved the rest. How many fish were left? For lunch, the polar bear ate three more fish. How many were left? At snacktime, he ate one fish. How many were left? For dinner that night he ate four fish. How many fish were left?

Jumpin' Rockhoppers

Rockhoppers are penguins that hop rather than waddle. Rockhoppers can jump as far as six feet on land. Share this information with the children in a small group. Then have the children see how far they can jump. Mark off a six-foot section with masking tape or secure a tape measure to the floor. Then have each child in the group stand at one end of the section and jump with both feet together. Mark behind the child's heels to show how far he jumped. Continue until everyone in the group has had a turn. Compare the distance a rockhopper can jump with the distance each child has jumped.

Rising To New Heights

Emperor penguins, which nest only in Antarctica, are the largest of all penguins. They can grow to be four feet tall. Share this fact with your class. Have each child compare his height with that of an emperor penguin. Attach a life-sized drawing of an emperor penguin to a wall. Measure each child using a roll of adding-machine paper. Cut off a strip of the paper equal to the child's height, write his name on it, and attach the strip to the wall beside the penguin drawing. Repeat this procedure for each child in the class. Compare and contrast each child's height with that of the emperor penguin.

How Many Scoops?

Try this fun-filled activity and your youngsters can imagine that they are measuring snow. Collect several transparent containers of various sizes and shapes. Mark "fill lines" on the containers by putting a piece of tape on each one. Place the containers, bowls of uncooked rice, and several detergent scoops in a learning center. Before pouring rice into a container, ask each child in the center to estimate how many scoops of rice it will take to fill each container to the tape line. As you fill each container, have the children count the number of scoops nccdcd to fill the container. Have them write the number of scoops on a scrap of paper and place it in front of the container. Ask the children to sequentially order the containers by volume.

3 scoops   6 scoops

A Cotton Ball Match

Obtain several small paper bags. Put between one and 20 cotton balls in each bag. There should be two or more bags with each chosen number of cotton balls. Let each child choose a bag of cotton balls and find a spot on the floor to sit down. Have him open the bag and count the number of cotton balls inside the bag. Ask four or five children to walk around the room and find the classmate or classmates with an equal number of cotton balls. When each child finds his partner or partners, have all of the children empty their bags onto the floor and line up their cotton balls for one-to-onc matching. Continue the activity until everyone has found a classmate with the same number of cotton balls. Counting cotton balls will seem like snowballs of fun!

165

LANGUAGE ARTS

A Polar Language Experience

Read *Polar Bear, Polar Bear, What Do You Hear?* by Bill Martin, Jr. Have the children create a similar book using all polar animals. Place several pictures of polar animals in a learning center (children's science magazines are a good source for these pictures). Talk about the sounds each animal makes. Ask the children to dictate sentences similar to those found in Bill Martin's book. One child might dictate the sentences, "Penguin, Penguin, what do you hear? I hear a snowy owl hooting in my ear." Another child may dictate, "Snowy Owl, Snowy Owl, what do you hear? I hear a seal barking in my ear." Write each pair of sentences on a sheet of chart paper. Let each child choose an animal to illustrate. Write or have the child copy the appropriate sentence on her drawing. Bind the pages together to make a class book.

Penguin, Penguin, what do you hear?

I hear a snowy owl hooting in my ear.

Initial Consonant Sounds

Sometimes polar animals have to cross cold Arctic rivers to reach their destination. Ask the children in a learning center to pretend an Arctic river runs through the middle of the center. Then place alphabet cards over the make-believe river. Have each child cross the river by saying a word that begins with that letter before stepping on a card. If the child fails to name a correct word, have him try again.

Polar Peekaboo

Duplicate the peekaboo patterns on page 172 for each child in the class. Cut each sheet in half. Use an X-acto knife to cut out the eyes. Give each child a copy of both halves of the worksheet. Have him draw a large picture of a polar animal vertically inside the rectangle. Have him place the completed drawing under the page with the cut-out eyes. Have each child write his name at the bottom of his paper. Collect both sheets from each child. Bind the papers together to make a class book, making sure each polar animal picture is beneath the eyes cutout. When sharing the book with the class, only a portion of each picture will be visible through the eye holes. Have the children guess the animal before turning the page to show it.

Critical Thinking

What physical characteristics help protect polar animals from the bitter cold? Have the children keep this question in mind as you read aloud several factual books and magazine articles about polar animals. Let the children assist you in making a list of the physical characteristics: several layers of fat, thick fur or feathers, water-resistant fur or feathers. Have the children think of the ways that people protect themselves from the cold weather. List the ideas on chart paper as the children dictate. Then have the children cut pictures of people in cold weather out of old magazines. Have each child share her picture with the class and describe what the person in the picture is doing or wearing to stay warm.

Vary the activity by asking the children to sit in a circle on the floor. Give each child one picture of an animal (some polar animals and some other animals). Have each child name her animal and tell if it would make a good polar animal. Have her explain why or why not by describing the physical characteristics that would or would not insulate the animal from the Arctic cold.

Polar Animal Vocabulary

Cut out several pictures of polar animals (penguin, polar bear, puffin, snowy owl, Arctic fox, caribou, walrus, Arctic hare, etc.). Glue the pictures to a large piece of poster board. Write the name of each animal under its picture. Attach the poster to a wall or bulletin board in a learning center. Then write the name on a sentence strip of each polar animal. Cut apart each name, letter by letter. Place the letters for each name in a separate plastic sandwich bag. Place the bags in the learning center and have the children in the center use the poster to help them sequence the letters in each polar animal's name.

SCIENCE

Shadows

Read *Shadow Bear* by Joan Hiatt Harlow. To demonstrate how shadows are formed, have the children sit in a circle on the floor and place a teddy bear in the center of the circle. Shine a bright flashlight on the bear to create shadows of various sizes and shapes. Talk about how the position of the flashlight beam affects the shadow of the bear. Then divide the class into groups of three. Give each group a sheet of white construction paper, a pencil, tape, and a bag of Legos or small building blocks. Take the groups of children outside. Place a large piece of cardboard on the ground. Have each group tape their sheet of paper to the cardboard. Tell each group to stack the building blocks on the paper and carefully trace around the shadow of the blocks. Later in the day, take the children back outside and have them trace around the same block building again. Discuss how the shadows have changed and what caused the changes.

Camouflage

After reading aloud several factual books about polar animals, discuss with the children how these animals use camouflage to protect themselves. Make a learning center where the children can experiment with camouflaging. Cut several strips of different-colored construction paper. Place them in the center. Collect sheets of printed paper (wrapping paper, wallpaper, shelf paper) and place them in the center. Have the children match each paper strip to the sheet of printed paper that best camouflages it.

Crystal Garden

Growing a crystal garden in your classroom will resemble an icy glacier in Antarctica. Cover the bottom of a disposable tin with charcoal briquettes. Mix together a solution of 1/4 cup salt, 1/4 cup bluing, and 1/4 cup ammonia in a glass jar. Place a few drops of food coloring on each briquette. Pour the salt solution over the briquettes and place the tin in a warm place. Crystals will start to form on the briquettes in a short time. In two days, mix another batch of the salt solution and pour it over the briquettes to grow more crystals.

A Popular Polar Snack

At the conclusion of the Polar Animals unit, let the children enjoy a polar snack of popcorn balls and juice.

Popcorn Balls

1/4 cup margarine
1/2 cup sugar
1/2 teaspoon salt
1/2 cup light corn syrup
8 cups popped popcorn

Heat the first four ingredients in a large saucepan until boiling, stirring constantly. Reduce heat and pour popcorn in the pan. Continue to stir until the popcorn is thoroughly coated. Cool slightly. Shape into three-inch balls and place the balls on a piece of waxed paper. Cool completely and serve or wrap in plastic wrap for later. One recipe makes 10 to 12 popcorn balls.

SOCIAL STUDIES

Directional Hide-And-Seek

Write the words *North, South, East,* and *West* on separate pieces of paper. Tape the words to the corresponding walls in the classroom. Show the class a toy polar animal or a picture of one. Select a child to leave the room. Ask another child to hide the toy animal. Have the first child come back into the room. Have her choose several classmates to help her find the animal. Each child chosen will give one directional clue. One child might say, "Take three steps north." Another might say, "Turn west." When the animal is found, another child is selected to leave the room and the game begins again.

Parent Penguins

Emperor penguins nest only in Antarctica, where the mother and father emperor penguins share the responsibilities of caring for their young. After the mother penguin lays her egg on the ice, she goes out to sea to feed. The father penguin takes care of the egg while the mother is gone. He carefully rolls it onto his feet and covers it with the lower part of his stomach. Then he huddles with other father penguins to keep warm. The mother penguin is gone for about eight weeks. During that time, the father penguin continues to keep the egg warm. He will not even leave to eat. Just after the egg hatches, the mother returns and the father goes out to sea to feed. He returns in about three weeks to help feed and care for the baby chick.

Share the information about emperor penguins with the children, and then discuss the duties and responsibilities they share with adults at home or at school. For homework, have each child work with a parent to write a sentence about one of the jobs she helps with at home and illustrate it. A child might write "I empty the garbage when it is full." The next day, each child can share her sentence.

I load the dishwasher after dinner.

ART

Paper Penguins

Make several tagboard patterns using the penguin pattern pieces on page 173. Place the patterns and several sheets of construction paper in a center. Have each child in the center trace around the pattern pieces to make a paper penguin. Have him use black paper for the body (tracing with white crayon or chalk), white paper for the stomach and eye, and orange paper for the beak and feet. Have him cut out the parts of the penguin and glue the pieces together to make a paper penguin.

Polar Scene

Place a variety of white odds and ends in a learning center: drinking straws cut in small pieces, corrugated cardboard, Styrofoam packaging materials, buttons, cotton balls, and yarn. Give each child in the center a Styrofoam meat tray. Have her make a polar scene by gluing some of the white objects on the tray. Have her make small polar animals from scraps of colored construction paper and add them to the scene.

Snowy Polar Paintings

Have each child in a learning center color a picture of a polar animal on a sheet of light blue construction paper. Mix together a solution of half water and half Epsom salts. Have each child use a paintbrush to paint a thin coat of the solution over his picture. As the picture dries, the salt crystals left on the paper will glisten like falling snow.

SNACK

Polar Bear Claws

1/2 banana for each child
1 round cracker or cookie for each child
Spreadable cream cheese
Flaked coconut

Slice the banana into sections. Spread the cream cheese on the cracker. Arrange the cracker and banana sections on a paper plate as shown so they look like a polar bear's claws. Sprinkle them with coconut.

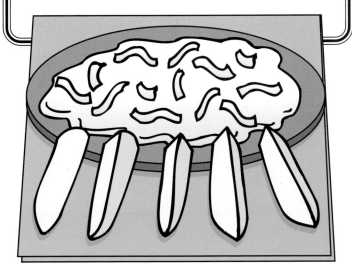

CULMINATING ACTIVITY

Polar Trip

On the last day of the unit, have the children pretend to take a trip to the polar regions. Ask each child to wear something white to school to represent snow and ice. Then read aloud *Little Polar Bear* by Hans De Beer. Next have your class dance to Hap Palmer's "Funky Penguin" from *Movin'*. Finally let the children enjoy a polar snack of popcorn balls (see the recipe on page 168) and juice.

Polar Animals Patterns

Use these patterns with "Polar Peekaboo" on page 166.

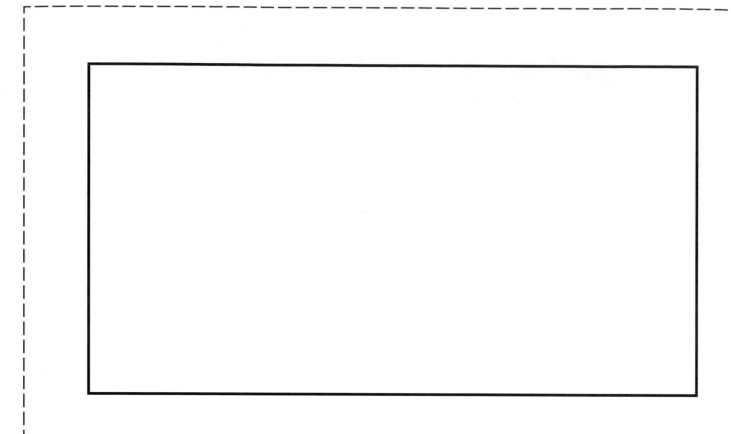

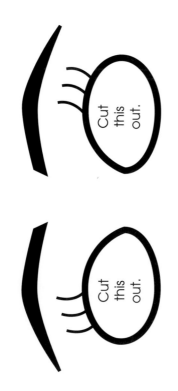

Cut
this
out.

Cut
this
out.

 ©The Education Center, Inc. • *Themes to Grow On* • *Fall & Winter* • TEC60799

beak

eye

foot

stomach

Polar Animals Patterns
Use with "Paper Penguins" on page 170.

foot

body

©The Education Center, Inc.

©The Education Center, Inc. • *Themes to Grow On* • *Fall & Winter* • TEC60799

173

Valentine's Day

Hearts are red; violets are blue; celebrate Valentine's Day with something new. Involve your children in enjoyable activities that strengthen friendships and build self-confidence.

MATH

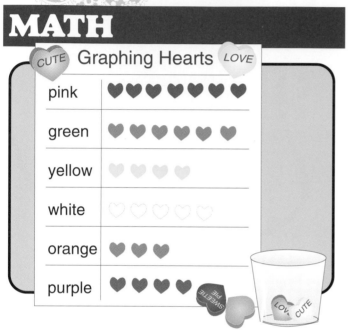

Graphing Hearts

CUTE	LOVE
pink	♥♥♥♥♥♥♥
green	♥♥♥♥♥♥
yellow	♥♥♥
white	♡♡♡♡♡
orange	♥♥♥
purple	♥♥♥♥

Conversation Hearts

Youngsters will surely enjoy this sweet hands-on graphing activity. Provide each child with a blank grid and a small cup of candy hearts. Ask him to sort the hearts by color. Then have him graph his assortment of conversation hearts. Have each child interpret and explain his graph. Allow your students to eat the hearts after this fun-filled activity.

Paper Bag Hearts

Write the numbers 1 through 10 on individual heart cutouts. Place the hearts in a small brown paper bag. Then, in turn, have each child reach in the bag and pull out a heart. The child with the lesser number is the winner. Let the children place the hearts back in the bag, shake it up, and play again. To vary the activity for older children, have each child take two hearts from the bag and add the two numbers together. The child with the lesser sum wins.

Heart Roll

Pour a bag of candy conversation hearts into a clear container. Place the container and a die with numerals in a learning center. Have the children in the center take turns rolling the die and removing the correct number of hearts from the container. Let the children continue to play until all of the hearts are gone. Then have each player sort his hearts by color and decide who has the most of each color. Finally let players decide who has the greatest amount of total hearts.

Numbers In Sequence

Give each child a copy of the reproducible on page 182. Have him fill in the missing numbers on the number chart.

174

Kisses And Hugs

Place a stamp pad, paper, and *X* and *O* rubber stamps in a learning center. Have the children in the learning center create original patterns of *X*s and *O*s. If rubber stamps are unavailable, let the children use markers.

Heart Hunt

Cut out 20 red hearts, ten pink hearts, and five white hearts. Program the red hearts with the numeral 1, the pink hearts with the numeral 5, and the white hearts with the numeral 10. Then hide the hearts throughout the classroom. Let your children go on a heart hunt. Tell them a red heart is worth one point, a pink heart is worth five points, and a white heart is worth ten points. When all the hearts have been found, have each child total her score by counting by tens, fives, and ones. The child with the most points is the winner. To vary this activity for younger students, program the hearts with numerals of lesser value and/or picture cues.

Heart Cards

Separate the jokers and the numbered heart cards from a deck of playing cards. Then prepare a poster listing an activity for each heart card (see below). Attach the poster to a wall in the center. Have the children sit in a circle. Place the cards in a stack facedown in the middle of the circle. Let the children take turns removing the top card from the stack and performing the corresponding task printed on the chart. When all the cards have been removed from the stack, shuffle the cards and begin the game again. Note: Simple drawings picturing the suggested activities could be drawn on the activity chart for younger children.

ace—Turn around once.
2—Pull ears twice.
3—Clap hands three times.
4—Pat head four times.
5—Jump five times.
6—Touch knees six times.
7—Hop seven times.
8—Touch floor eight times.
9—Raise hands nine times.
10—Pat tummy ten times.
joker—Do all ten activities.

LANGUAGE ARTS

Heart Messages

Cut several hearts from construction paper. Print a valentine word such as *love* or *heart* or a message such as *be mine* or *I love you* on each heart. Have each child in a small group choose one heart. Then let him place a piece of cardboard under his heart and use a pushpin to punch holes in each letter. Caution your students to be very careful when using the pushpins. Afterwards hang the hearts in a window. The light will shine through the holes, creating sunny messages.

Valentine Concentration

Purchase a box of children's valentine cards. Select several matching pairs of valentines from the box and glue each valentine to an individual index card. Laminate the cards for durability. Then have the children in a learning center place the cards facedown in the center of a playing area. Let each child take a turn turning over two cards. If the cards match, the child keeps them. If they do not match, the cards must be turned facedown again. At the end of the game, the player with the most matching pairs is the winner.

Heart Directions

Give each child in a small group a copy of the reproducible on page 183. Then read the following set of directions and have the children follow them:

1. Draw an arrow through the first heart.
2. Draw lace around the second heart.
3. Draw a happy face inside the third heart.
4. Draw stripes on the fourth heart.
5. Color the fifth heart red.

Next let each child in the group make up directions for completing one of the remaining hearts and have the others follow them.

Broken Hearts

Cut several heart shapes from red construction paper. Write an uppercase letter on the left side of each heart and the corresponding lowercase letter on the right side. Then cut the hearts in half for youngsters to match. To vary the activity, program the halves with compound words, color words/color dots, or *up* and *down* pictures.

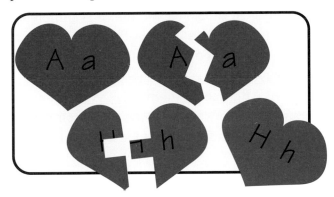

Valentine Poetry

Print the following traditional poem on a sheet of chart paper or large heart cutout. Read the poem aloud with your children. Then ask them to think of words they could substitute for *roses, violets,* and *sugar.* Print the revised poem on another piece of chart paper or large heart cutout and read it aloud with your children. Repeat the procedure several times to create different versions of the same poem.

Roses are red.
Violets are blue.
Sugar is sweet,
And so are you!

Roses are red.
Violets are blue.
Sugar is sweet,
And so are you!

Apples are red.
My eyes are blue.
Honey is sweet,
And so are you!

Firetrucks are red.
Skies are blue.
Chocolate is sweet,
And so are you!

Secret Valentines

Write each child's name and address on a slip of paper. Fold it and put it into a container. Let each child take a slip of paper from the container and read to himself the name of his secret valentine. Then have him make a card for that person. Next have him write his valentine's address on an envelope and place a stamp in the corner (ask each child to bring one stamp from home prior to the activity). Once the valentines are finished, make a list of each student's secret valentine. Have the school's letter carrier pick the valentines up from your children. Your classroom will fill with excitement in a few days when the children tell of the valentines they have received in the mail.

The Jolly Postman...

Read *The Jolly Postman Or Other People's Letters* by Janet and Allan Ahlberg to a small group of children. Then discuss the various letters, cards, and advertisements sent to the different fairy-tale characters. Next have the children work together to make similar letters, such as one from Snow White to the Seven Dwarfs or one from the shoemaker to the elves. Print each letter on a sheet of chart paper as it is dictated by the children. Then copy the letter onto a small sheet of white construction paper and have a child illustrate it. Bind the letters together to create a class book.

SCIENCE

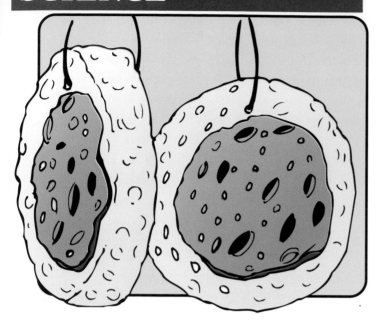

Birdseed Valentines

Read "Thousands Of Valentines For Hundreds Of Friends" by Susan M. Paprocki, from *Short-Short Stories* compiled by Jean Warren. Then have your children make a valentine for the birds. Place a quantity of rice cakes, pieces of flexible wire, plastic knives and a jar of peanut butter, and a container of birdseed in a learning center. Have each child in the center thread a piece of wire through the top of a rice cake and twist it to make a hanger. Then spread peanut butter on one side of the rice cake. Next sprinkle birdseed over the peanut butter. Hang the birdseed valentines on a tree outside your classroom and watch the birds enjoy them.

Heart Smart

Invite a cardiologist, pediatrician, or school nurse to talk with your class about the most important muscle in the body—the heart. Ask him or her to discuss how eating the right foods and getting the proper exercise can strengthen the heart. Then let each child use a stethoscope to listen to her heartbeat. Finally let your children sing along with Slim Goodbody's "Lubba-Dubba" from the CD or cassette *The Inside Story.*

Healthy Heart

The American Heart Association—in conjunction with the American Alliance for Health, Physical Education, Recreation, and Dance—has developed *Jump Rope for Heart,* a two- to four-week program designed to educate schoolchildren about cardiovascular health while raising money for vital research. The program encourages teamwork and shows children that physical fitness can be fun. It is complete with instructional aids, a wealth of additional materials, and much more. For more information about *Jump Rope for Heart,* contact the American Heart Association. After the program, have your youngsters brainstorm the ways they can keep their hearts healthy. Write their dictated responses on a large heart cutout.

A Beating Heart

Use this activity to show your children how their heart rates increase when they exercise. Play a quiet song and ask your youngsters to move slowly to the music. Afterwards tell them to feel their hearts with their hands. Then play a fast song and have your children dance to it. Let them feel their hearts again. Ask the children to tell if their hearts are beating faster or slower than before. Next play another slow song and instruct the children to move slowly around the room. Have them check their heart rates when the song is over. Finally tell your youngsters to sit still and listen to one last quiet song. Again ask them to feel their hearts and tell if they are beating faster or slower. Then ask children to explain why.

Be Heart Smart

SOCIAL STUDIES

Field Trip

Arrange a time when your class can visit the local post office for a tour of the facilities. If a tour of the post office is not possible, invite the school letter carrier to visit your class. Have him or her discuss the duties and responsibilities of his job. Then ask him to mail the class valentines (see "Secret Valentines" on page 177).

Post Office Center

An activity that is sure to be popular with your children is the Post Office Center. The center may be as elaborate or simple as time will allow. Listed below are some of the items that may be included:

- a desk, small table, or puppet stand for the counter
- a cardboard shoe organizer or several empty shoeboxes for sorting the mail
- junk mail donated by parents
- gummed stickers to be used as stamps
- play money
- a date stamp and stamp pad
- an old, light blue shirt to be worn by the mail carrier
- a canvas tote bag for carrying the mail
- an index card for each child with her name and address printed on it
- envelopes, masking tape, self-sticking labels, small cardboard boxes, and pens

Have the children in the center take turns pretending to be the mail carriers and customers. Let each customer copy her name and address on an envelope and take it to the postal counter to be mailed. Each customer may also wrap a package using the masking tape and an old cardboard box. The address may be copied onto a label and attached to the box. Allow each student to use the stamp pad and date stamp to program her envelope. The mail carriers can sell stamps, sort the mail, and deliver the mail to the proper locations.

ART

Valentine Zoo

Make a variety of animals using paper hearts (see examples). Attach the animals to a wall in a learning center for the children to use as models. Then cut out or die-cut hearts of all sizes from sheets of pink, white, and red construction paper. Place the hearts, glue, and a quantity of black markers in the center. Then have the children use the materials to make valentine animals. Tell your youngsters they may copy your examples or create their own animals. Attach the animals to a bulletin board and title it "Valentine Zoo."

Mend A Broken Heart

Give each child in a small group a sheet of red construction paper and a large heart pattern. Have him trace around the pattern and cut out the red heart shape. Next cut the heart into several pieces. Then put it together again on a white background, leaving a little space between each piece. Once the broken heart is in place, glue it to the background paper. Next attach the heart picture to a larger piece of pink construction paper to make a frame. To decorate the frame, dip the end of a pencil eraser and the prongs of a fork in red and/or white tempera paint to create a design.

Valentine Card

Fold a pink sheet of construction paper in half to create a card. Then cut out a half-heart from a piece of red construction paper that is smaller than the card. Glue the half-heart shape and the paper from which it was cut to the front of the card as shown so that the two pieces form a heart.

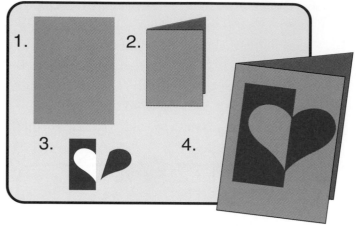

A "Heart-y" Basket

Make a cute "heart-y" basket for your students to use to hold their valentines. To make a basket, cut two large hearts of equal size from red or pink construction paper. Staple the hearts together around the sides and bottom as shown. Staple an end of a paper-strip handle inside each top side of a heart. Have your youngsters decorate the baskets with glitter or glitter glue, markers, or paper lace doilies.

SNACK

Heart Cake

Prepare a cake mix according to package directions. Then separate the batter into one round cake pan and one square cake pan. Bake the cake and cool it completely. Then place the square cake on a large platter with one corner pointing downward. Cut the round cake in half. Place each of the halves as shown to make a heart. Ice the cake with canned frosting and decorate it with candy sprinkles.

CULMINATING ACTIVITY

Valentine's Day Party

Plan a very special Valentine's Day party. Place the valentines in a large canvas bag. Then invite the school's mail carrier to come and distribute the cards to your students. If the mail carrier is not available, ask the school principal or a fellow teacher to dress up like a mail carrier and do the honors.

Valentine's Day
Number Chart

Use with "Numbers In Sequence" on page 174.

1				5		
		10			13	14
	16		18		20	
22			25	26		
	30			33		35
		38			41	
43	44					49

©The Education Center, Inc. • *Themes to Grow On* • *Fall & Winter* • TEC60799

1

2

3

4

5

6

7

8

9

Snow

This avalanche of ideas will fill your classroom with the sparkle and excitement of a first snowfall!

MATH

Keep Counting

Make several copies of the snowflake pattern on page 191. Cut out the snowflakes and then laminate them. Use a hole puncher to punch a different number of holes in each one. Tell the children to be ready to count the holes in each snowflake. Place a snowflake on an overhead projector screen. Then turn the projector off quickly. Have the children tell how many holes they saw in the snowflake. To check, turn the projector on and count the number of holes in the snowflake. Repeat the procedure with another snowflake. Vary the activity by allowing pairs of students to use the snowflakes and projector in a learning center.

Cotton Ball Counting

Make a large gameboard similar to the one pictured. Place the gameboard and a basket of cotton balls in a learning center. Have the children in the center sit in a circle around the gameboard. Give each child a button and a small paper bag. Explain the rules of the game. In turn, each child should toss a button onto the gameboard. If the button lands on a numeral, the child takes that many cotton balls from the basket and places them in his paper bag. If the button lands on a line or goes off the card, the child gets another turn. When each child has had five turns, the game ends. The child with the most cotton balls in his bag is the winner.

Snowflake Patterning

Give each child a copy of the small snowflake patterns on page 192. Let her color each row of snowflakes using two different crayons to make a pattern. Have her cut the rows apart on the dotted lines. Collect the rows of snowflakes from every child and attach them to a wall or bulletin board.

Numerals

Make a poster similar to the diagram below. Place the poster, several crayons, and paper in a learning center. Have the children in the center follow the printed directions to draw a picture of a snowman.

For older children, substitute number words for numerals.

Make 3 circles.

Make 2 eyes.

Make 1 nose.

Make 2 arms.

Make 4 buttons.

Make 1 hat.

Make 1 mouth.

Make 1 scarf.

Matching Mittens

Supply each child with a pair of mitten cutouts and some crayons or colored pencils. Show the children several pairs of wool or cloth mittens. Describe the symmetry used to make both mittens match. Have each child design a pair of matching mittens. Encourage the children to use stripes, dots, and other designs to make the pairs of mittens unique. Have each child write his name on the back of each mitten. Collect the mittens and place them in a learning center. Mix up the mittens and then have the children in the center match the pairs.

Time Melts Away

Give each child in a learning center a plastic sandwich bag. Place an ice cube in each bag and seal it shut. Tell the children they will participate in a race to see who can melt her ice cube first. Have them think of creative ways to melt their ice cubes. Use a minute timer, a stopwatch, or a second hand on a clock to time the race.

LANGUAGE ARTS

Compound Words

After discussing and reading about snow and snow-related topics, explore snow-related compound words with the class. Print the word *snowman* on a sheet of chart paper. Print *snow* and *man* beside *snowman* to show the two parts that make the whole. Have the children think of other snow compound words: *snowsuit, snowflake, snowball, snowstorm, snowfall, snowshoes, snowdrift, snowplow, snowbird,* and *snowcap.* List each word on the chart as children dictate. Have each child choose one of the compound words and make a simple book. Give her three sheets of paper and have her write the first part of the compound word on one sheet of paper and illustrate it. Then have her write and illustrate the second part of the compound word on the second sheet of paper. Have her write the compound word on the third sheet of paper and illustrate it. Bind the three sheets of paper together to create an individual book. For younger children, write the words on each page.

Sequencing

Read *The Mitten* by Jan Brett to your youngsters. Have the children name the eight animals in the story that use the mitten as a temporary home. You may want to write the name of each animal in sequential order on the chalkboard as it is dictated by the children. Give each child a copy of the sequencing pictures on page 192. Ask him to color the pictures and cut them apart. Give him a mitten cutout and have him glue the pictures on the mitten in sequential order.

A Snowman Language Experience

Discuss the steps involved in the creation of a snowman. List the steps on chart paper as the children dictate. Have each child illustrate one of the steps on a sheet of paper. Write the sentence that goes with the illustration at the bottom of each paper. Older children can copy the sentence from the chart. Bind the sheets together to make a class book.

First make 3 big snowballs.

Place the snowballs on top of each other.

Letter Recognition

Use the snowflake pattern on page 191 to make several snowflakes from poster board. Write an uppercase letter on the left side of each snowflake and the corresponding lowercase letter on the right side. Cut the snowflakes apart to make each self-checking. Place the halves in a learning center. Have the children in the center match the uppercase letters to the lowercase letters by putting each snowflake together. Vary the activity by programming the snowflakes with number words/numerals, color words/color dots, or rhyming pictures.

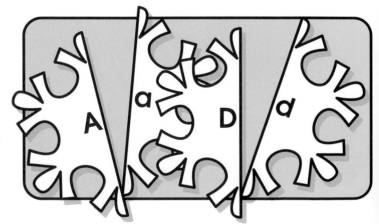

SCIENCE

Snowfall Prediction

When will be the first snowfall? Will it be morning, afternoon, or night? Will it come at the beginning, middle, or end of the month? When the snow comes, will it cover the ground? How deep will it be? Brainstorm the answers, or predictions, to these questions with your children. Record each response on a calendar. If you live in an area where it does not snow, have your class predict the next rainfall or ice storm.

Properties Of Water

Demonstrate how water changes form with the following experiment: Pour one cup of ice in a saucepan. Heat the pan on a hot plate. Have the children describe how the ice changes form as it is heated. Heat the remaining water to a boil. Have the children describe the changes in the water as it is heated.

Evaporation

Fill a glass jar half full of water. Mark the water level. Place the jar in a sunny window. Mark the water level each day until all of the water has evaporated. Have the children tell where the water went. Call their attention to the sediment left in the bottom of the jar. Discuss with the children why the sediment was left in the jar.

Melting Ice

Allow the children to experiment with ice and the factors that determine the rate at which it melts. Fill three clear plastic cups that are the same size as follows: Fill one cup with water and freeze it until solid. Fill the second cup with ice cubes and the third with crushed ice. Place the three cups of ice on a table in front of your class. Have the children estimate which container of ice will melt first, second, and third. Write the children's responses on chart paper. Have the children estimate when the ice in each container will melt and record their responses. Older children may give their estimations in hours and minutes. Younger children may decide if the ice will melt before lunch, after playtime, before center time, etc.

Vary this activity by filling three clear plastic cups with the same amount of ice cubes. Place the cups in different locations around the classroom. For example, place one cup of ice in a window, one under a bright light, and one inside a closet. Have the children estimate which container of ice will melt first, second, and third.

Which Will Melt First?

frozen solid	Joe	Lori	Chris			
ice cubes	Cathy	David	Jay			
crushed ice	Morgan	Kevin	Loni	Alex	Nancy	

SOCIAL STUDIES

Maps

Show the children several examples of simple maps. Discuss the important parts of each map. Draw a simple map of a town on the chalkboard or on a large sheet of paper. Draw some of the major features such as roads, railroad tracks, lakes, and an airport. Have the children suggest various types of buildings that might be found in the town (school, hospital, police station, fire department, library, post office). Then draw them on the map.

Follow up the introductory map activities by reading aloud *Katy And The Big Snow* by Virginia Lee Burton. Review all of the people and places Katy helped during the snowstorm. Have the children make a map of the town Katy helped. In a learning center place the following items for a map-making project: construction paper, glue, scissors, crayons, chalk, toothpicks (optional), tempera paints, and Legos. Also include a large piece of cardboard for the base of the map or tape together several sheets of poster board. Have small groups of children take turns making the following different areas of the map:

Paint the cardboard base with green tempera paint to represent grass and brown tempra to represent bare ground. Use blue tempera paint to add a lake to the scene.

Glue black strips of construction paper to the map to make roads. Use chalk to draw the center lines on each road. Glue a gray strip of paper near the location for the airport to make a runway.

Glue narrow strips of brown construction paper to the map to make a railroad. Ties can be made using additional strips of brown paper or toothpicks.

Use Legos to make the buildings Katy helped in the story. Place them in appropriate locations on the map.

After the map is completed, have the children use toy vehicles and Styrofoam packing pieces for the snow to dramatize the story.

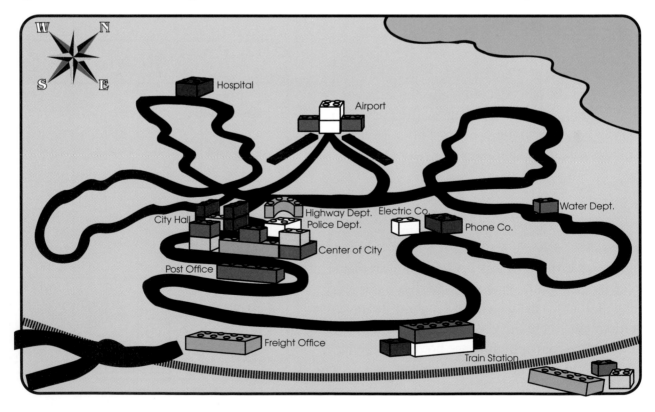

ART

Snow Puff Painting

Your youngsters will enjoy making a snowman with puff paint. To make puff paint, in a medium-sized bowl mix equal parts of flour and salt. Divide the mixture into several smaller containers. Make a pasty substance by adding a different color of liquid tempera paint to the mixture in each container. Pour the paste into plastic squeeze bottles. Place the squeeze bottles of puff paint, several sheets of blue construction paper, containers of white tempera paint, and round sponges in a learning center. Have each child in the center make a snowman on a sheet of construction paper using a sponge dipped in the white paint. Then have her use the squeeze bottles of puff paint to add features to the snowman.

Snowball

Give each child in a learning center a four- or five-inch square of cardboard and some white yarn. Have him wind the yarn around the cardboard square so that it is completely filled. Have him carefully slide the cardboard out from inside the yarn and gather the yarn in the center. Tie a small piece of yarn tightly around the center. Have him use scissors to cut the yarn loops. Fluff the cut loops to make a ball. The yarn snowball can be used in a tossing game.

Mosaic

Have each child in a small group make a snowman mosaic. Give her a large sheet of white construction paper. Have her draw a large circle and a smaller circle for the snowman's body. Have her cut out both circles. Then have her cut both circles into strips either horizontally or vertically, keeping the strips in order. Glue the strips in the correct order on a large piece of blue construction paper, leaving space between each strip. Have her use paper scraps to make the clothing and features for the snowman.

Crayon Resist

Have the children in a learning center make original snow scenes using crayon resist techniques. Give each child a sheet of light blue construction paper and several waxy crayons. Have her use the crayons to color a winter scene on the paper. Emphasize the importance of solid coloring. Place small containers of diluted white tempera paint and paintbrushes in the center. Have her carefully brush the tempera paint over the crayon drawing to create the effect of snow.

SNACK

Hot Cocoa Mix

1-lb. box Nestle's Quik
8-qt. box instant nonfat milk
6-oz. jar nondairy creamer
1 cup powdered sugar

Mix together the ingredients and store the mix in an airtight container. For one serving, add two tablespoons of cocoa mix to one cup of hot water and stir. Let the cocoa cool some before serving.

Let each child make a snowman stirring stick to use with his cup of hot cocoa. Push a plastic stirring stick through two or three marshmallows. Give each child three chocolate chips to make the snowman's eyes and nose. Have each child use a dab of frosting to make the chocolate chips stick to the marshmallows. Have him stir his warm cocoa with a snowman and enjoy.

CULMINATING ACTIVITY

Snow Globe

Crush eggshells into very fine pieces and place them in a container. Put the container of eggshells, mineral oil, the small objects listed below, and glue in a learning center. Then give each child in the center a clean peanut butter or pickle jar with a lid. Have her choose from several of the following small objects to glue to the inside of the lid: stones, plastic winter figurines, moss, sticks, pinecones, etc. Let the glue dry for approximately 30 minutes. Then let each child fill her jar with mineral oil and add some of the eggshells. Finally have her screw the lid on the jar securely, shake the jar gently, and watch the "snow" fall.

Snow Pattern

Use with "Keep Counting" on page 184 and "Letter Recognition" on page 186.

©The Education Center, Inc. • *Themes to Grow On* • *Fall & Winter* • TEC60799

Snow Patterns   Use with "Sequencing" on page 186.

©The Education Center, Inc.

©The Education Center, Inc.

©The Education Center, Inc.

©The Education Center, Inc.

©The Education Center, Inc.

©The Education Center, Inc.

©The Education Center, Inc.

©The Education Center, Inc.

Use with "Snowflake Patterning" on page 184.

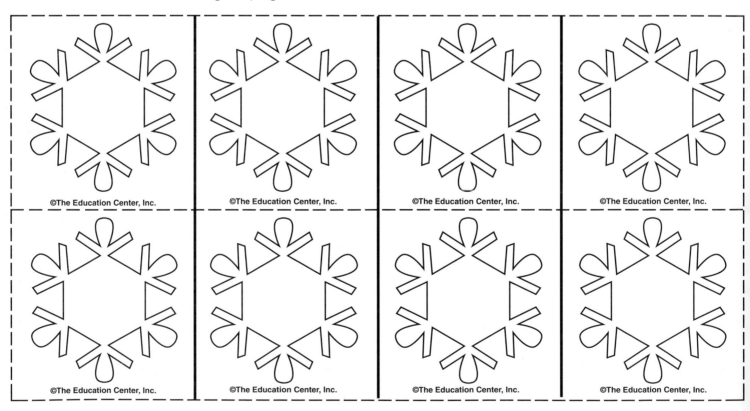

©The Education Center, Inc.

©The Education Center, Inc.

©The Education Center, Inc.

©The Education Center, Inc.

©The Education Center, Inc.

©The Education Center, Inc.

©The Education Center, Inc.

©The Education Center, Inc.

©The Education Center, Inc. • *Themes to Grow On* • *Fall & Winter* • TEC60799